Politics of Maturity

Politics of Maturity

Tanya Loughead

LEXINGTON BOOKS
Lanham • Boulder • New York • London

Published by Lexington Books
An imprint of The Rowman & Littlefield Publishing Group, Inc.
4501 Forbes Boulevard, Suite 200, Lanham, Maryland 20706
www.rowman.com

86-90 Paul Street, London EC2A 4NE

British Library Cataloguing in Publication Information Available

Library of Congress Cataloging-in-Publication Data

Names: Loughead, Tanya, author.
Title: Politics of maturity / Tanya Loughead.
Description: Lanham : Lexington Books, [2023] | Includes bibliographical references and index.
Identifiers: LCCN 2023021085 (print) | LCCN 2023021086 (ebook) | ISBN 9781666907261 (cloth) | ISBN 9781666907278 (ebook)
Subjects: LCSH: Maturation (Psychology) | Social history. | World politics. | Equality. | Justice.
Classification: LCC BF710 .L68 2023 (print) | LCC BF710 (ebook) | DDC 155.2/5—dc23/eng/20230602
LC record available at https://lccn.loc.gov/2023021085
LC ebook record available at https://lccn.loc.gov/2023021086

∞™ The paper used in this publication meets the minimum requirements of American National Standard for Information Sciences—Permanence of Paper for Printed Library Materials, ANSI/NISO Z39.48-1992.

Contents

Acknowledgments vii
1 What Is Maturity? 1
2 Psychoanalytic Approaches to Maturity 9
3 Failure and Immaturity 31
4 Maturity as a Political Project 47
5 The Family Is a Political Structure 65
6 Maturing as Critical Openness 87
Bibliography 101
Index 107
About the Author 113

Acknowledgments

This book was written in the midst of struggles: the global COVID pandemic, Women's Marches, Black Lives Matter protests. At my place of work, there were massive layoffs, salary and benefit cuts—part of a vicious regime of capitalist austerity imposed on millions of working-class people from steel mills to universities. We must never forget: In organizations where hierarchies exist, workers will always be vulnerable to economic violence and injustice. But the world can be *otherwise.*

I hope everyone who picks up this book is in the midst of organizing and creating or strengthening a union. I thank my comrades Becky Krawiec and Girish Shambu for hours, weeks, and years of conversation about ideals, futures, failures, and tactics. I also thank my comrades in the Jesuit Higher Ed Labor Coalition, the Western New York Faculty Coalition, and the American Association of University Professors.

It is in direct struggle that we often learn the deepest lessons, and that has been the case for me over the past five years. Small-minded, unreflective people can and do rise in stature and power. This is as true in university or corporate boardrooms as it is in the police force or government. I am reminded regularly that success in this world often has nothing to do with maturity.

I thank those who edited and proofread earlier versions of these chapters: Mairead Farinacci, Ana Grujić, and (especially) Sarah Torbeck.

I also thank my comrades in the Radical Philosophy Association and the Phenomenology Roundtable. Hashing through ideas with you all at conferences strengthened arguments and broadened ideas in this book.

For camaraderie, dancing, sharing vegan meals and wine, and many spirited conversations, I am indebted to: Alexander Bertland, Jon DiCicco, Ana Grujić, Adrienne Hill, Dan Jamros, Ami Lake, Sarah Pierce and Jasmina

Tacheva. I also thank my neighbors—Cammie, Anna, Kelly, Kathy—shrewd and funny creatures who enrich life.

To those with whom I household: Doru, Girish, Epi, Wallace and Seemers . . . gratitude. I will not use the word "family" here (a point to be explained in this book!), but we share daily and nightly living—living full of humor, riley dialogue, wonder, affection, and, sometimes, logic.

Chapter One

What Is Maturity?

"We know that whatever answer we give, it will be wrong."

—Carlos Sanchez[1]

The question of maturity is ripe for philosophical analysis. We each have some type of "common sense" or "intuitive" grasp of what maturity is since we believe ourselves to experience it—a grasp that may turn out to be misguided. We know that our common sense is often simplistic and ideological and that philosophy can help us figure out how or why.

What is maturity? As the epigraph suggests, it is hard to answer this question, but my purpose here is not to offer a definitive answer. Instead, I wish to add to a conversation about what the process of maturing should be. If, in this book, my oversights and failures are productive or interesting, I shall consider that good. Adam Phillips once posed this question: "What can we say to each other if neither of us needs to be right?"[2] Philosophy as a discipline will benefit (and mature!) to the degree that it takes this question seriously. It is a question that Friedrich Nietzsche asks when he writes in *Beyond Good and Evil*, "What in us really wants truth?"[3] This is not to imply that saying something true is not important, nor is it to believe that any lie is acceptable as long as it gets us where we want to go (a kind of pernicious and simplistic pragmatism). Rather, it means: Let us say what we can on an issue from the perspective we occupy, and let us welcome disagreement and contradiction. Donna Haraway once warned, "But by the time you reach the end of a sentence, you've said at least six things that aren't true and you don't hold, but to get to the end of the sentence you don't have any choice. You can't simply say what you mean—that's not how language works."[4]

Maturity has usually been dealt with in two insufficient ways: 1) as an issue of individuals, individual personality, and growth, and 2) as the sole province of psychology or psychoanalysis. To my knowledge, there has been no thorough philosophical analysis, no speculative theorizing, of the maturing process. Philosophy often assumes that we are rational, conscious, mature subjects. Our epistemological theories, theories of mind, ethics, and conceptions of justice deal almost without exception in terms of fully formed, emotionally stable (or emotionless) human beings who can make various "choices" in their lives, including the choice to know. The human being is a chooser. What is the right thing to do, the thing that our rational, mature subject would do? Who is this imaginary philosophical subject? He is not me and I do not know him. The human beings we know (and are) are all at vastly different levels of maturing. Therefore, philosophy needs to talk about maturity. To put this in "virtue ethics"-speak, Aristotle says that courage is the enabling virtue, that without courage one cannot practice any other virtue. But I would claim that the enabling virtue is in fact *maturing*, and we should be working to create a society in which its movements are actively fostered.

When we consider our friends, family members, lovers, coworkers, politicians, bosses, and so forth, we often believe that we can judge who is more or less mature. *Why can't my coworker just grow up?* By which we might mean: Why can't he be more like me? Why can't he follow expectations and norms? Why can't he be more successful in the world? We must admit at the outset that this way of thinking—conflating maturity with normative ideas of success—is difficult to avoid. An even more difficult trap when thinking about maturity is assuming a teleological, goal-oriented approach. The term maturity itself calls to mind ideas of *telos* and progress. According to Anna Tsing, "progress stories have blinded us."[5] Like Tsing, I want to warn us against teleological narratives of progress, although it is difficult to think outside of them entirely since "most of us were raised on dreams of modernization and progress."[6] This contradiction between modernist ideas of ever-expanding progress and the materialist world we inhabit must cause a rupture in our understanding and urge us toward more imaginative possibilities.

We are all in a state of precarity, humans and nonhumans both, albeit not to the same degree, as we collectively experience the catastrophic effects of climate crisis. It then becomes increasingly silly to speak of progress, as our rational selves know that this is no longer possible, if it ever was. In Tsing's words, "Now it seems that all our lives are precarious—even when, for the moment, our pockets are lined. In contrast to the mid-twentieth century, when poets and philosophers of the global north felt caged by too much stability, now many of us, north and south, confront the condition of trouble without end."[7] Tsing invokes the geologists who refer to our time as "the Anthropocene, the epoch in which human disturbance outranks other geological forces" and concludes that "without planning or intention, humans have made a mess of our planet."[8]

The good news (and here I agree with philosophers like Shulamith Firestone and Simone de Beauvoir) is that there is nothing about our supposed species nature that made this mess (or this belief in a teleological progress) inevitable. We are not stuck in that way of living; we can choose to live and to think otherwise. Prompted to think beyond epistemically and imaginatively impoverished narratives of progress, Tsing asks philosophical (and scientific) questions about how we can learn to live in ruins: What new ways of conceptualizing ourselves and our world will carry us forth into our unknown catastrophic future? Her approach leads to mushrooms that have adapted and thrived in human ruins; can *we* figure that out? This might sound grim to some, yet it is reality. Not only are our past ways of living and thinking no longer viable, we need to admit that they were never sustainable, nor were they just.

How, then, can we move in a direction of adaptive development (but not "progress" in the usual sense) that allows us to live and perhaps thrive like Tsing's mushrooms in a different kind of world? We must do this, knowing that our old definitions and concepts (including the concept of maturity) have brought the collective home of our species and millions of other species to ruin.

How can reflecting on our own maturing process and the perception of others' maturity lead us to critiquing society and questioning its structures? It is clearly not possible for a person to mature all by themselves. Therefore, the accusation that "he's an immature jerk" is *not only a judgment against an individual but also an entreaty for social change.* Society is not doing the work that it should: We are not structured in such a way that we can safely and openly be in a state of becoming and maturing with and among others. But we are also defining maturity in quite a misguided way. Such a faulty concept in turn provokes what I understand to be immature behavior. This, then, is not just a problem of individual psychologies but an issue for philosophers and activists. In other words, the lack of maturity in a society is not merely a statement about individual personalities, it is also a political and philosophical statement requiring analysis.

In this book, I use conceptual tools from critical theory and psychoanalysis to help frame the issue articulated above and to raise some fundamental questions. Leftists and philosophers in general have not always been comfortable with psychoanalysis as a legitimate approach to knowledge. Louis Althusser said in a letter meant to defend an article on psychoanalysis that he deliberately chose to publish it in a French communist journal (which was noted for referring to psychoanalysis as "a reactionary ideology") because "no theory of psychoanalysis can be produced without basing it in historical materialism."[9] I agree with Althusser on this point and broaden it to say that no theory of maturity can be produced without basing it within a historical materialism of class, race, sex, sexuality, ability, and other political structures. Gilles Deleuze describes the subject by way of a "fold" where the social and political exterior is folded to the interior of the subject: What is outside is always embedded inside the subject.[10] Our social and political context is the ground for all of our development and expansions, or our lack of them, our stagnancy and closure.

Too often we separate these two intertwined issues: political/social matters, on the one hand, and individual maturity, on the other. It is hard not to notice when we engage in activist work that we encounter people who are not at all mature. As one of my Facebook friends said in response to a *New York Times* piece on men in therapy after #MeToo,[11]

> One of the most off-putting experiences of academia and radical politics was realising that even the most radical of male PhD candidates, tenured academics or activists were still mostly just posturing little boys, with the emotional intelligence of lobsters, who treated women like shit. I don't think political consciousness can bypass or precede the important need for "growing the fuck up" emotionally and mentally. And this is very personal work, it is a necessary precondition for radical collectivity. Too often in radical circles personal growth work is de-privileged in favour of grand political conceptualisation, and the end result is a bunch of mean children playing at being radical with all the same toxic (non-existent) interpersonal skills.[12]

Indeed. Working together with others requires that we work on ourselves as individuals as well. We might need to be wary of being "woke" or maybe even "radical" itself, as this can also imply that one has reached a state of political enlightenment and consciousness when all work on oneself can cease. The underlying assumption is that intellectual growth will necessarily be accompanied by all other types of growth. Yet, as my friend noted, we all know "accomplished" people who are nonetheless "posturing little boys."

In sum, this project grounds maturing as an inherently political project. We all mature within a context, and where that context contains hierarchies, inequalities, and oppressions, they will affect all of us, both the oppressed and the privileged.

Let us start with a provisional definition of maturity. The standard contemporary Western notion of maturity is teleological, assuming that "adult" is a stable position to be achieved. This position entails completing such tasks as developing the skills that the market desires, acquiring a well-paying full-time job, getting married, buying a house, procreating, and generally understanding and achieving one's capitalist and familial expectations. Additionally, being perceived as an adult may involve leaving behind the amusements and creative pursuits one once enjoyed so that life may revolve around work and/or family. An adult is a pragmatist, a tool who serves capitalist goals: Staying up late to finish a report for work is adult, whereas staying up late with friends is not adult. However, we should also say that these capitalist and familial expectations shift depending on one's identity, whether one is a man or a woman, for instance. Many people think that being a proper adult man requires making money and acting as a leader, but would they define a proper adult woman in this way?

Normative maturity is the demand of replication. Replicating the past is what Hannah Arendt calls non-thinking. She describes time as a line moving from the past through us and into the future, where the easiest thing to do is to carry on with the line. Even to say "carry on" is too active for what Arendt implies, as it is more like taking a ride on a moving train on which intentional activity is limited.[13] Sara Ahmed, too, critiques the reproduction of the past in "the form of family love, expressed as the demand to return such love through how one loves: in other words, the love that you receive, narrated as the gift of life, converts quickly into a pressure to continue the 'good lines' of the family."[14] Thus, being "mature" is about continuing the love that your family gave you in the same way they gave it. Ahmed speaks about how "the prohibition of miscegenation and homosexuality belong, as it were, in the same register": family love.[15] Of course, your family may no longer love you if you do not replicate their lives by forming a heterosexual couple with someone of your race, background, and class, getting married, and having biological children with them. Jack Halberstam writes of "values, wealth, goods, and morals [being] passed through family ties from one generation to the next,"[16] which sounds like the "bad/habitual life" that Arendt describes: replicating the past without much thought.

We notice the same cultural expectations patterned not only in the two examples that Ahmed gives but in other places, too, such as when someone (especially a woman) chooses not to have children and people deem this "selfish." If maturity is replication, then we can see how it becomes understood that it is selfish and immature not to replicate what previous generations did; it is an improper use of the love invested in you by your family. Take as another example the many times young White men from "good families" are charged with crimes like rape but the judge is concerned that the ruling might ruin the man's future and replication of an unending, unchanging line of sameness, which is fundamentally what a "good family" means. Even being a rapist should not get in the way of a man being able to replicate the goodness of his family.[17]

My working definition of maturity is quite the opposite of these capitalist and familial replicative achievements. We will start with this: Those who are maturing make themselves open and porous to the world by way of critical and active thinking. This is not teleological, for there is not some definable point at which peak maturity has been reached. Indeed, we are more likely to recognize immaturity than maturity. We can recognize immaturity as sets of behaviors, emotions, and reactions in people who seem closed, defensive, stubborn, selfish, acquisitive, and living in bad faith and ideology without an openness to questioning. Just as Jacques Derrida says that justice is always "to come,"[18] here we shall say that maturity is always to come, something to reach for and never fully grasp.

In *One-Dimensional Man: Studies in the Ideology of Advanced Industrial Society*, Herbert Marcuse writes that we can think about concepts as having either a transitive meaning or an operational meaning.[19] Concepts that we understand to be transitive we treat dialectically; we relate them politically to the concrete world, and thus these concepts shift in understanding as the world itself changes or as we want the concepts and the world to change. As Marcuse puts it, "All cognitive concepts have a transitive meaning, they go beyond descriptive reference to the particular facts"[20] and "critical philosophical concepts refer (no matter how indirectly!) to alternative possibilities."[21] On the other hand, for Marcuse, "operational concepts" are divorced from the concrete world and its potential changes. Such a concept is used in order to conform individuals to the way society is. It is a closed concept lacking imaginative possibilities. An operational concept is "false to the extent to which it insulates and atomizes the facts, stabilizes them within the repressive whole."[22]

The concept of maturity is often treated as an operational concept. We use the word freely as if we already know what it means and how it operates in our lives. Not only should we seek clarity about what maturity is, but we need to go further, beyond the goal of clarity. I intend in this work to redefine maturity in overtly political terms. It is not merely my goal to get to the bottom of what everyday people mean when they talk about maturity. Perhaps a more analytic philosopher would do this. The goal of clarity and understanding would also have an "ideological and political character," but one that might go unnoticed. Because that type of analysis reflects our current society, it (typically unintentionally) assumes that our society is basically good, with concepts worth saving and promoting. That is not my view. In this work, I argue for a liberation through redefinition. In Marcuse's words, "Dialectical thought understands the critical tension between 'is' and 'ought,'" and we must have "consciousness of the discrepancy between the real and the possible."[23] By engaging in a critical analysis of maturity, we go beyond the given form of society and reach toward what *might* and *ought* to be rather than *what is.*

POSSIBLE PITFALLS

By way of setting our path for the rest of the work, I indicate a few pitfalls that I think we should try to avoid when thinking about maturing:

1. We must not fall into teleology, and yet one cannot entirely escape a teleological-like approach. It is helpful to use Derrida's distinction between *archaeological* (a structure, an origin/system) and *eschatological* (full presence, end of time) movements.
2. We will not characterize all lack or all anxiety as signs of immaturity. Sometimes anxiety can provoke a movement toward openness.
3. We will not conflate age (the passage of time) with maturity.
4. We will not presume that maturity is the same in all times or cultures or that the experiences, opportunities, or effects are the same regardless of gender, race, class, sexuality, etc. We will avoid notions of maturing that do not take historic and material conditions into consideration.
5. We will not presume that those individuals who are normatively "successful" in a given time or culture (those who make a lot of money, become leaders, celebrities, or government officials, etc.) are mature. We deny the link between success and maturity since that link presumes that the values a society embodies are themselves mature. Nor will we assume that those who are less successful by normative measures are necessarily immature.

NOTES

1. Carlos Sanchez, "Ortega y Gasset's Existentialist Critique of Husserl's Transcendental Phenomenology," presented at the 15th Annual Meeting of the Phenomenology Roundtable, California State University Fresno, May 24, 2015. Quoted with permission of Carlos Sanchez.
2. Adam Phillips, at a Week-Long Residency with Adam Phillips at The Center for the Study of Psychoanalysis and Culture, SUNY-Buffalo, 2015.
3. Friedrich Nietzsche, *Beyond Good and Evil: Prelude to a Philosophy of the Future*, trans. and commentary by Walter Kaufmann (New York: Vintage Books, 1989), 9.
4. Donna J. Haraway, "Companions in Conversation (with Cary Wolfe)," in *Manifestly Haraway* (Minneapolis: Minnesota University Press, 2016), 209.
5. Anna Lowenhaupt Tsing, *The Mushroom at the End of the World: On the Possibility of Life in Capitalist Ruins* (Princeton: Princeton University Press, 2015), viii.
6. Tsing, *The Mushroom at the End of the World*, 20.
7. Tsing, *The Mushroom at the End of the World*, 2.
8. Tsing, *The Mushroom at the End of the World*, 19.

9. Louis Althusser, *Writings on Psychoanalysis: Freud and Lacan* (New York: Columbia University Press, 1996), 31–32.

10. Gilles Deleuze, *The Fold: Leibniz and the Baroque*, trans. Tom Conley (London: Athlone Press, 1993).

11. Avi Klein, "Opinion: What Men Say About #MeToo in Therapy," *New York Times*, June 30, 2018, https://www.nytimes.com/2018/06/30/opinion/sunday/men-metoo-therapy-masculinity.html.

12. Ivan Niccolai, on the Facebook page of Jaleh Mansoor, July 10, 2018. Quoted with permission.

13. Hannah Arendt, "Thinking and Moral Considerations: A Lecture," *Social Research* 38, no. 3 (Autumn 1971), https://www.jstor.org/stable/40970069.

14. Sara Ahmed, *Queer Phenomenology: Orientations, Objects, Others* (Durham: Duke University Press, 2006), 127–28.

15. Ahmed, *Queer Phenomenology*, 127.

16. J. Halberstam, *In a Queer Place and Time: Transgender Bodies, Subcultural Lives* (New York: New York University Press, 2005), quoted in Sara Ahmed, *Queer Phenomenology: Orientations, Objects, Others* (Durham: Duke University Press, 2006), 85.

17. In the Brock Turner sexual assault case, there was much hand-wringing about what the rape conviction would do to Brock's future, with a judge in the case saying in 2016 that he worried that a prison sentence would have a severe impact on it (see EJ Dickson, "Why Are Judges so Concerned About the Future of Potential Rapists?" *Rolling Stone*, July 19, 2019, https://www.rollingstone.com/culture/culture-features/judge-james-troiano-brock-turner-sexual-assault-855415/). We saw this in the 2018 Brett Kavanaugh confirmation hearings as well: How dare a woman speak against a man's character when he was doing such a good job of maturing, going to prep schools and ivy league schools as his ancestors did, marrying a woman of his class, getting a respectable job, procreating, and getting promotions along the way. Can't we all see how very mature and responsible he is, ticking all the boxes? He could never be a sexual assaulter with such a solid record of replication. And even if he is, that's no reason to ruin the forward trajectory of his "good family."

18. Jacques Derrida, "Force of Law: The Mystical Foundation of Authority," in *Deconstruction and the Possibility of Justice*, ed. Drucilla Cornell, Michel Rosenfeld, and David Gray Carlson (New York: Routledge, 1992), 27.

19. Herbert Marcuse, *One-Dimensional Man: Studies in the Ideology of Advanced Industrial Society* (Boston: Beacon Press, 1991).

20. Marcuse, *One-Dimensional Man*, 106.

21. Marcuse, *One-Dimensional Man*, 217.

22. Marcuse, *One-Dimensional Man*, 107.

23. Marcuse, *One-Dimensional Man*, 133, 229.

Chapter Two

Psychoanalytic Approaches to Maturity

"For psychoanalysis, it is axiomatic that we never fully know who we are."

—Jacqueline Rose[1]

The border between philosophy and psychoanalysis is no border at all. Both fields ask questions about what the human mind is, how it functions, and what its health, illness, flourishings, or failures might be. Similarly, it makes little sense to split fields like sociology and psychology since no one has a psychology in a room by themselves and there is no sociology without human minds and behaviors. But philosophy is (or ought to be) ideal for asking the foundational questions that often go assumed in other fields. Certainly, those in the field of psychology have dealt with the issue of maturity (or "development," as they are more apt to call it) more than have those in philosophy. In this work, I have chosen to include some discussion of psychoanalysis. I shall not be engaging with the field of psychology (as it is normatively known in the United States) except through psychoanalysis. I have two reasons for this: 1) every project must have boundaries, and mine shall be to discuss Sigmund Freud, Donald Winnicott, and other psychoanalysts who deal with the unconscious and with the social creation and anthropology of subjects; 2) I do not believe that the conceptual tools of behaviorism or positivist psychology are enough to provide satisfying answers to my questions. As Winnicott admonishes, straightforwardly psychological approaches to the matter do not explore the unconscious. "I am concerned with unconscious motivation," he writes, and this cannot be properly discovered with a machine or a computerized questionnaire; in this case, Winnicott says, "those who have spent their lives doing psychoanalysis must scream out for sanity against the insane belief in surface phenomena that characterizes computerized investigations of human beings."[2] I primarily focus on the work of Freud and Winnicott in this chapter not because I think that they are the only psychoanalytic approaches worth studying but because I find in their work the most with which to agree, disagree, and illustrate points that I wish to foreground about maturing. For me, the field of psychoanalysis is rich with deep connections to philosophy and a philosophy of maturity.

In *Progressive Psychoanalysis as a Social Justice Movement*, Scott Graybow writes that many within this movement maintain that psychoanalysis treats people as "whole persons" whereas "manual interventions such as cognitive behavioral therapy (CBT) are limited by their ability to do anything more than provide brief symptom remission"; according to Graybow, CBT "risks being nothing more than a form of shallow positivism . . ."[3] It is not an accident that positivist forms of American therapy are on the rise at the same time as neoliberal capitalism, according to writers such as Neil Altman, who maintains that understanding race, sex, class, and other relational structures is key in the therapeutic process. One would think that discussing these systemic issues within a therapeutic setting would be a norm, as they impact most people's daily lives; after all, we are not generic human beings, and our "identities" are always political. However, Altman describes how much of the current "technology of psychology" is narrowly focused on the "separable individual" and is thus antithetical to the beliefs fueling broader social justice aims. In fact, under our capitalist healthcare structures, such narrow approaches to therapy can contribute "to the oppression of the poor and other marginalized communities who have little choice when seeking mental health assistance but to submit to 'time limited, narrowly goal-oriented, and cost-efficient focused psychotherapy and medication-based treatments.'"[4] On the other hand, according to writers such as Graybow and Altman, psychoanalysis tries to get to the roots of issues—roots entwined with structural and political imprints on subjects—rather than merely treating symptoms. It would take another book to fully flesh out the distinctions between psychoanalytic and positivist therapies; I am merely hinting at why psychoanalysis holds some promise for us in trying to understand and reshape the processes of maturing in rich and politically complex ways.

With this in mind, let us look at some of what Freud has to say about maturing.

FREUD ON THE MATURING PROCESS

Freud describes the maturing process by way of an analogy about the archeology of a city: Layers get added as we mature, but the old layers still exist underneath the present layer.[5] The layers of the self that Freud has in mind are, in the order in which they are formed, the id (the primordial, oceanic state of self and the world not yet separate, pure pleasure), the ego (separation of the self from the world, protection of the self, negotiating reality while minimizing pain), and the superego (internalized discipline, social norms, guilt). Freud explains the construction and the relationship of these layers: "The adult's ego-feeling cannot have been the same from the beginning. It must have gone through the process of development."[6] Of the emergence of the ego layer from the id, Freud writes, "An infant at the breast does not as yet distinguish his ego from the external world as the source of sensations flowing in upon him. He gradually learns to do so, in response to various promptings."[7] The infant learns that their body is separate from the world and thus, in Freud's language, moves from the pleasure principle (what Freud describes as an "oceanic" feeling of being one with the world) to including the reality principle (understanding separation enough to learn to avoid pain coming from the outside world in order to protect the self). Freud continues, "Originally, the ego includes everything,"[8] since the infant knows no separation, and "our present ego feeling is, therefore, only a shrunken residue of a much more inclusive—indeed, an all-embracing—feeling which corresponded to a more intimate bond" between the ego and the world.[9]

Therefore, by Freud's reckoning, a mature person contains all three layers of the self. Obviously, these layers are not stable like they would be in the archaeology of a city. Throughout a person's life and experiences, all three layers can alter, shift, and permeate each other, and the relationship between them can shift, too. A perfect example of a possible shift is the process of going through analysis, which should open the patient to understanding these layers and the destructive ways they may be relating to one another. Analysis—when it works—can help one to catch a fleeting glimpse or hint at the reasons why one acts, sees, or thinks in the way one does, and this knowledge itself ought to open one up. Or, in the words of Julia Kristeva, "no modern human experience aside from psychoanalysis offers man the chance to restart his psychical life and thus, quite simply, life itself, opening up choices that guarantee the plurality of an individual's capacity for connection."[10]

The reason I emphasize this shifting between the layers is that while maturity may seem to be a finished project, once one reaches the level of superego, this does not imply a stasis or the subject's unchangeability, according to Freud. Since our experiences are always adding to and shifting who we are, the connections we can make at the various levels of self could be continually expanding. Or, given a traumatic experience, the self might revert and contract. Any analyst must begin with the idea that experiences shift our psyche, and as long as we are experiencing, we are potentially maturing.

The ego is not as stable as one might think, as Freud further theorizes: "Normally, there is nothing of which we are more certain than the feeling of our self, of our own ego" as "something autonomous and unitary, marked off distinctly from everything else." While this is partly true, it is also "deceptive,"[11] for there are times in a person's bodily and mental life when "perceptions, thoughts and feelings" might "appear alien to him and as not belonging to his ego"; there are "other cases in which he ascribes to the external world things that clearly originate in his own ego."[12] Freud concludes that ". . . even the feeling of our own ego is subject to disturbances and boundaries of the ego are not constant."[13]

Even though Freud is describing the individual psyche, an individual is never entirely separate from others, the border between self and others being porous and unstable. If we look at each layer of the psyche according to Freud, we can see that each is related to the outside world and to others. The id wants to be one with the world, the ego wants protection/defense against the world, and the superego wants to know how live up to social norms in the world. At every level, there are relationships to others.

FREUD ON SEXUALITY'S ROLE IN MATURITY

According to Freud, one cannot avoid talking about sexuality when outlining the maturing process. Many people make an assumption that sexuality does not exist for the individual until puberty, that sexual desire is "absent during childhood."[14] Freud distinguishes the sexual *object* from sexual *aim* and says that "we have assumed a too close connection between sexual instinct and sexual object."[15] What this means is that we assume that sex has to do solely with reproduction and must be 1) centered on the genitals only, and 2) heterosexual. In fact, human sexuality has never been only about this, and Freud shows how, even in the most vanilla sex, there is still much that, strictly speaking, is not directed toward reproduction. For example, why do people kiss? If the supposed reason for all sexuality is egg meeting sperm, kissing is unnecessary. In another example, Freud asks why a woman's breast would be excited by touching and notes that the "touching in itself evokes a feeling of pleasure" while, at the same time, it "demands still more pleasure."[16] Freud directs his attention away from the assumed instinct-bind when he concludes, "How it happens that the perceived pleasure evokes the desire for greater pleasure, that is the real problem."[17]

Of course, if human sexuality were caused only by evolutionary reproduction, there would be no homosexual desire (what Freud calls "inversion")[18] or other desires outside the bounds of heterosexuality, across different times and cultures (and in other animal species, too). Nor would there be fore-pleasure, kissing, or looking, all of which are "perversions" to the reproductive act. In other words, Freud shows that sex is always more complicated than the reproduction of the species. Hence, we need to look beyond mere copulation for the sake of reproduction in order to have some grasp of the unlimited spectrum of human sexualities. In turn, if we assume that sexuality begins at puberty, we narrow all sexual desire and causation.

But the question remains: Why necessarily talk about sexuality when trying to understand maturity? Freud outlines two paths for maturity, depending on one's genitalia. How one matures is determined by the almighty penis, or whether or not one has it. He writes that "it is known that the sharp division between the male and female character is established at puberty"[19]—which seems odd considering that Freud has spent hundreds of pages talking about how we should not overestimate the importance of puberty as the cause and opening of sexuality. Why claim that puberty is not the start of sexual desire and at the same time that puberty is the start of gender differentiation? I would have expected Freud's critique of reproductive sex to continue and shape some of his critique of gender as sex. Surely, the various characters of females, males, and non-binary persons are all more complex than some genital awakening at puberty? Freud does lay the blame for this reductive differentiation at the feet of social repression: "If one wishes to understand how the little girl becomes a woman," puberty "brings to the boy a great advance in libido, distinguishes itself in the girl by a new wave of repression."[20] But why does a "boy" have a great advance of libido at this time? Why is Freud so sure that the "girl" does not? Freud blames this repression on the body, specifically the clitoris, but this seems wrong since a clitoris cannot cause repression while the psyche *can* do so via social expectations, that is, "civilization."

Throughout Freud's work on raising a child, the parent is assumed to be a woman (mother) and the child is assumed to be a boy: "For by teaching the child to love, she only fulfills her task" and "the child should become a capable man with energetic sexual needs."[21] Here, Freud seems to have some interest in upholding normative gender and sexuality roles. Etienne Balibar writes that, for Freud, "there is no 'natural' determination of sexual identity (masculine or feminine), but only an unconscious historical construction."[22] Yet Freud clearly discusses the clitoris and penis as the basis for character, what later philosophers like Simone de Beauvoir call a causal link between sex and gender. Balibar admits that "one might claim, Freud never gives up circumscribing preferred forms of identity in the course of a given 'development'" and that this development is a kind of "law that the individual must uphold in order to join the social order."[23] The result, according to Freud, is that girls and women are constantly seeking male attention and approval due to unconscious penis envy; both girls and boys build the three layers of the self (id, ego, superego) and go through the levels of oral, anal, and genital libido, but girls' egos and superegos will forever be more fragile and unstable. We can—and should—critique a genital-based approach to maturity that reifies gender. However, while avoiding the essentialism of gender roles, we should not too quickly deny the *descriptive* importance of Freud's work.

Fortunately, Freud speaks with many conflicting voices on this theme. Sometimes he openly questions feminine and masculine gender roles and the naturalness of heterosexual desire, and at other times he is conservative, essentialist. Clinical psychotherapist Ann Murphy notes that, on this matter, contradictions permeate psychoanalytic thinking "all the way back to Freud's radical, conflicted, disorderly, multiply revised" 1905 work "Three Essays on the Theory of Sexuality,"[24] also known as "Three Contributions to the Theory of Sex." According to Freud, it "is essential to understand that the concepts of 'masculine' and 'feminine' whose meaning seems so unambiguous to ordinary people, are among the most confused that occur in science" and that they do not exist purely in "either a psychological or biological sense."[25] However, Murphy notes, in other places Freud "backtracks" into gender and sex essentialism. She deems this the difference between the "radical Freud" and the "panicked Freud, who did not have the courage of his most revolutionary ideas."[26] I find such contradiction in so-called foundational texts a hopeful thing. It leaves a clearing for interpretive and clinical work. Of course, I side with the radical Freud: Let us have the courage that Freud himself could not muster.

WINNICOTT ON PLAY, REALITY, AND THERAPY

In the last chapter of his book *Playing and Reality*, Winnicott associates youth and immaturity with irresponsibility, idealism, and rebelliousness. His approach (at least in the last chapter) seems conservative. Here, becoming mature looks rather like stoicism. We learn to tell the difference between what we can change and what we cannot. We put away the toys of our youthful idealistic selves and pick up the cold rational tool of making do with what is. It gives some explanatory power as to why our political systems seem terrible and yet unfixable: Adults become cynical that any change is possible. The adult says, "It is childish to hope we'd ever have anything different! Work with the system we have!" This type of cynicism passes for "realism" (in the everyday meaning rather than the philosophical meaning of the word) and is shot through our contemporary society. Powerful forces keep it in place; our cynicism did not grow in our minds on its own. This is one reason why maturity is a political issue—too many people understand maturity to be *the acceptance of what is.*

What Winnicott portrays as maturity in his final chapter, I tend to understand as precisely the opposite: a sign of immaturity through a lack of reflection. The fear of failure; the fear that dreaming of a different world will keep you from normative success; the fear that what you might dare to hope is not possible; the fear that others will not understand you or share your views; the fear that you will be mocked . . . Might these be signs of immaturity? A maturing person is not limited to what *is* but instead possesses the curiosity, the freedom, and the open mind to think of what *could, might, or should* be. Winnicott's definition of maturity, on the other hand, can lead to apathy and bad faith. Worse, it favors shoring up the power relations that already function in a society. By default, it supports those power relations. Based on his last chapter alone, I would not accept Winnicott's version of what an adult is.

Luckily, his book contains other chapters with rich ideas. In a chapter called "The Place Where We Live," Winnicott argues that it is a narrow modernist idea to claim that individuals have some inner psychic reality where they progress in emotional growth. At the opposite end, we have a tendency to think only in terms of people's "behavior," limiting ourselves to observing only the externalized acts of others. Each side is flawed. This is a false split between the inner/mystical and the outer/supposedly objective. It is a third area, the "in between," that Winnicott is interested in—and where psychoanalysis operates.[27] For Winnicott, culture is a shared "in between" space, a space that is neither fully internal to the subject nor an external shared reality. (I have some reservations about his use of the concept of a wholly "external reality," but I leave those aside for the moment.) Winnicott critiques a psychoanalytic practice if it deals only or primarily with the inner reality, and his work on transitional objects is key here.

For Winnicott, psychoanalysis needs to theorize how a subject moves from interior ("me") to exterior ("not me") and to theorize what potential supports or problems arise in this movement. The transitional object is the original not-me thing to which a child becomes attached. This process has no gender distinction: Infants identified as girls and boys follow the same process and with similar objects, according to Winnicott. What is interesting is how the transitional object institutes *play*, the key concept of Winnicott's work, which I will soon discuss at greater length. Although scholars have tended to focus most on his notion of transitional objects, Winnicott emphasizes why play is so important to the functioning adult. Through the gradual maturing of the child, the transitional object loses its special meaning, which then becomes diffused over the whole territory between the inner and outer reality.[28]

In earlier life (prior to the transitional object), an infant holds the illusion that the external reality corresponds to their capacity to create. According to Winnicott, the "mother" supplies the infant with everything they need.[29]

(I put "mother" in quotation marks to call attention to the gender essentialism of his psychoanalysis. Male parents, adoptive parents, grandparents, siblings, nannies, neighbors, etc., also fulfill primary caregiving roles. Henceforth, I will use the word "caregiver" instead.) A caregiver's job is to cause a gradual disillusionment, a weaning from the belief that the external reality corresponds to the baby's creation. This disillusionment will continue with other caregivers and educators throughout the child's life.[30] Winnicott claims that "the task of reality acceptance is never completed, no human is free from the strain of relating inner and outer reality."[31] To summarize some of Winnicott's key ideas, growing up is gradual disillusionment, culture is a strain but also the site of our maturing, and, therefore, growing up will never be an entirely pleasant experience.

This makes one wonder at cultural objects experienced as frictionless pleasure. To make a broad (and therefore not wholly accurate) statement, the lack of friction in objects of culture may be a reason that people choose those objects, be they television shows, movies, music, video games, etc. These are often chosen specifically for their ability to cause a break from the tension in our lives. Culture that is familiar asks little of us and leaves us with few questions. One wonders whether Winnicott would consider such frictionless entertainment or pastimes (literally, ways of passing time before one must work again) to be culture, since it seems that, for him, culture is precisely that region where the inner and outer rub up against each other in ways that provoke the individual to question their self, their ideas, and their sense of what "reality" is.

Winnicott includes an interesting comment, almost a throwaway line, regarding the potential power of conversation that illustrates he has a modest notion of what psychoanalysis is—which is not to say that he thinks it is not powerful (or that other types of therapy are better, as he explicitly denies behaviorist/ego psychology types of therapy[32]). For Winnicott, psychoanalysis is merely one possible way of helping people reach the goals of culture and play if they have not been able to do so throughout a "healthier" maturing process. He gives the example of a patient, a young boy, who lived far away from the city in which Winnicott was a practicing therapist, such that regular visits from the boy would be impossible. In this case, Winnicott spoke with the mother and father of the boy and gave them some prompts and suggestions for conversation. This conversation alone (without psychoanalysis per se) helped the parents gain confidence in dealing with their child, and these conversations did, in a sense, cure or at least ameliorate the problem.[33] The story seems to powerfully suggest that deliberate, structured conversation can be a type of *culture* in the sense that it provokes the individual out of their self toward that in-between space that Winnicott proposes. Once that in-between space has been recognized, play is possible.

Play is in-between, neither fully inside nor fully outside the individual. But it does have a time and place. For instance, play within therapy takes place at the space of overlap of the patient's sense of play and the therapist's sense of play. If the patient is incapable of play, then the therapist must be directed toward trying to bring the patient to a place where they are capable of play.[34] Play exists in a precarious and delicate manner, a maneuvering between the subjective and objective. Winnicott's point about the therapist's duty to help patients become capable of play illustrates a broader point: *No one becomes capable of play on their own*. We learn to negotiate and become more complex in relating to that space as we mature emotionally. Winnicott makes this clear when he says that "a description of the emotional development of the individual cannot be made entirely in terms of the individual . . . in certain areas . . . the behaviour of the environment is part of the individual's own personal development and must therefore be included."[35]

We should not forget that the therapist is also a human person subject to emotional development and processes of maturing, not an objective robot performing various services. Winnicott brings attention to this several times in his text. In moments of humility and honesty, he says that it was only at a particular (later) stage in his own development that he was capable of attaining the insights that brought him to his book. He "needed to live through" certain experiences in order to arrive at his current understanding.[36] He also writes that within the therapeutic practice, therapy will not work if the therapist is not capable of play. The more capable of play the therapist is, the better that therapy (and, likely, all conversations) will go.[37] When a patient is speaking, a therapist should not interrupt or excessively try to organize and interpret the thoughts and ideas of the patient, for "the patient's creativity can be only too easily stolen by a therapist who knows too much."[38] For Winnicott, maturity in the therapist means that they "wait" until the patient arrives to a point of understanding "creatively and with much joy."[39] Winnicott admits, "I think I interpret mainly to let the patient know the limits of my understanding."[40] This confession reminds me of Socrates and his dialogical, questioning way of approaching theory. Perhaps Socrates was the first play therapist, among his many other characteristics, for he encouraged his "patients" to figure out the meanings of love and justice through his playful questioning. Both Winnicott and Socrates recognize the significance of allowing others the joy of discovery and uncovering. This paves the way for subjects to develop the courage and curiosity to engage with *friction-full* culture.

WHAT DOES IT MEAN TO LIVE LIFE CREATIVELY AND PLAYFULLY?

Winnicott defines play and creativity in a much broader way than is common, claiming that perception itself is a creative act. Creativity "refers to a colouring of the whole attitude to external reality,"[41] and, for him, "Creative apperception more than anything else" makes life worth living. This is the opposite of having a compliant relation to reality. Winnicott states that "Compliance is a sick basis for life" in which "nothing matters," whereas living creatively is a "healthy state."[42] Of course, the dichotomy is polemical here; there are no extremes to either side (creative vs. compliant), as just as in Maurice Merleau-Ponty's view there is no absolute objective or subjective but each is entwined with the other.[43] Winnicott sounds like Merleau-Ponty when he claims that play is neither inside nor outside.[44]

In Winnicott's view, external reality is not a mere projection of the subject.[45] Object-relating turns to object-use as the subject learns to place the object in a space and time *outside* of their omnipotent control. This balance, according to Winnicott, is the most difficult hurdle in maturing. He provides a related pedagogical dichotomy: A) a person who has "schizoid" tendencies, and B) a person so anchored in outside reality and its expectations that they have little subjectivity and no creativity. Directly relevant to our discussion, Winnicott explains that children and babies are closer to "A," the subjective, schizoid side, although we would never use the word "schizoid" to describe them since they typically develop and mature out of it.

In Winnicott's account of maturing, in the earlier stages of human history, living creatively was rare and compliance was expected and the norm. Thus, maturing was a matter of moving from the subjective/schizoid state of being a baby toward objective/external reality in a society that demanded compliance of "mature" adults. Certainly, this kind of expectation lingers in our contemporary society. When people associate "adulting" with activities like getting married, buying a house, and having kids, these are sets of expectations that act as markers for recognizing an adult. People who choose to opt out of these activities are mocked for "playing" too long (e.g., "playing the field" by resisting monogamy), for refusing, like Peter Pan, to grow up. Over the past decade, countless think pieces have proclaimed that millennials do not buy houses at the rates of earlier generations because they refuse to engage in the proper rituals and lifestyles indicative of maturing. One hears that those who frequent parties, eschew marriage and/or parenthood, enjoy sex with multiple partners, live in a city as opposed to the suburbs, or have too much fun (or eat too much avocado toast) are not properly adults. In this dominant narrative, being an adult is serious business, not "fun," not "play."

Here we might be able to interpret parts of Winnicott's version of maturity as standing in contradiction with the normative one. Winnicott believes that maturity requires play. For him, a person incapable of play is a person who lives inside compliance, possibly a neurotic who pays too much attention to social expectations and markers.

Norman O. Brown argues that the difference between those deemed "healthy" and those deemed "neurotic" is that the former have a socially useful form of neurosis.[46] Yes, most of us are neurotic, but some people's particular strain of neurosis is useful to the economy, the role expected of them due to race or gender, and so forth. This is what much normative therapy tries to do: take those people with types of neuroses that do not serve the system and turn them into people whose neuroses are profitable. We might consider a related example: Some feminist scholars point out that the beauty-industrial complex profits precisely by encouraging women to feel insecure about their physical appearance. If women are confident without being "beautiful" in some normatively narrow way, they are not useful to the economy.

Loosely following the practices of Freud and Winnicott, a therapist typically starts with a neurotic (those who seek therapy the most) who has anxiety issues that often involve the defense of the ego. Therefore, therapists often think of "healthy" as a state in which the defenses are not rigidly held up; a healthy person is one who is open and flexible. Yes, but, Winnicott asks, what does health look like? What is life about? And here we return to the idea at the start of this chapter, that psychoanalysis and philosophy must be related. When we seek to have better relations in the world, to be happier or more fulfilled in life, what does that actually mean? Neurotic patients do not inspire this question because the goal is to help them become less rigid, but psychotic patients *do* inspire this question. Why should one leave the subjective to focus on the outside world, the space between the inner and outer? Why should one engage with culture? Winnicott claims that the mature person recognizes that we can only be original with regards to a tradition.[47] Creativity means to engage with what is; hence, the psychotic is never really original or creative. The creativity of a neurotic is stifled, too, since they are overwhelmed with the expectations, norms, and traditions of the outer world. But what Winnicott seems to add that is new is that *neither the neurotic, nor the psychotic is capable of play*. Play requires the subject (an inner life) to be engaged with the outer world and with culture. The more aware and engaged with culture one is, the more creative one might become. A state of health, play, and openness toward maturing is somewhere in the middle of these two imaginary poles.

Let us explore this implied link between psychotics and children: immaturity. Winnicott knows that adult neurotics are more likely to seek therapy because they seek more connection, freedom, flexibility, and relatedness in life. Adult psychotics, on the other hand, are less likely to seek therapy as they may not see the need and may be generally satisfied with their subjective/inner world. How, then, does one persuade psychotics that they should live differently than they do? Should they? The question is important because, if Winnicott is right, then that question is similar to this: How does one persuade children (or people in general) to "grow up"? These are complicated philosophical questions about what a person is, how one ought to live, and whether we have foundational responsibilities toward others.

Once we state that to be a child is to be linked to a kind of subjective, psychotic existence, a wrong/problematic implication could be drawn. One can be "immature" and wrapped up in a subjective world if one believes that being entirely compliant to the objective world is what constitutes being mature. This, of course, would imply that the neurotic is the most mature person. The more neurotic, the more mature! One imagines someone entirely anxious about complying with norms in the external world. In reality, this is not Winnicott's trajectory. Healthy development should exist in some middle ground of culture, of forever negotiating the inner and outer worlds in more complex, open, and fascinating ways.

Winnicott speaks of the act of identification with others and, in so doing, comments on Jacques Lacan's "mirror stage." Lacan claims that the baby first begins developing an ego when they see the mother's face, that the mother's face is the first mirror. Winnicott says that when babies see their mother's face, they see themselves.[48] Once again, caregivers (plural) is a better word to illustrate my point. Hopefully, many people are caring for the baby, and even with one primary caregiver, a baby sees the faces of many people and animals, so there is no reason for Winnicott (or psychoanalysis) to reduce the "face" to that of the mother. Winnicott states that, in certain cases, "the main hope of the therapist is to increase the patient's range in respect of cross-identification."[49] I agree, and I suggest that a maturing and ethically developing person will cross-identify with many faces, human and otherwise. Therefore, let us expand Winnicott's analysis to other caregivers, friends, and living beings. For instance, our circle of identification widens when a diversity of lives, races, sexualities, genders, sizes, ages, and abilities are represented in media; if heroes and complex characters are predominantly light-skinned, thin, straight, cisgender, and male, it affects everything about how we see them and those who are not represented as heroic or complex. This matters a great deal if, as Winnicott states, identification is such an important part of the maturing process. Or, consider the efforts of the activist group Toronto Pig Save, which performs direct actions that reveal the ethical depth of cross-identification. Animal rights volunteers stand by the side of the road at the entrance of a slaughterhouse and, as trucks full of live pigs approach, the volunteers push bottles through the slats of the trucks to give the pigs a drink of water, which the pigs receive gratefully. The volunteers take videos of the pigs, focusing on eyes filled with worry and fear. They identify the fear, discomfort, and thirst of the pigs through understanding their own similar feelings.

Let us look at how Winnicott directly discusses maturity. He offers a list of issues as signposts of development.[50] "Autonomy" is the goal, he writes, as is being able to independently take care of oneself. I have serious reservations about this. This idea, shared by many, of self-sufficiency as the indication of achieved maturity harms us all; it is a value prevalent in men especially, as a "real man" does not need anyone to take care of him,[51] and the value also leaves out or infantilizes differently-abled or neuro-divergent people. It can lead to a libertarian ethic of "each man for himself," a universe that, strictly speaking, is not possible for any of us. We all depend on thousands of others. At this very moment as I write at my local coffee shop, I depend on the person who brewed my coffee, the producer of my coffee cup, the workers who crafted the table at which I sit, the computer builders and software developers who made it possible for me to type on this machine, and many more. Karl Marx noted that a belief in self-sufficiency is not only false, it leads to alienation; capitalism creates multiple types of alienation, including alienation from our fellow human beings.[52] Thus, we should be cautious with Winnicott's notion that one must be self-sufficient to be mature. While Winnicott does admit that the movement from full dependence to independence is never total,[53] I believe, going further, that a maturing subject recognizes their *interdependence*.

Nevertheless, there are many aspects of Winnicott's theories on maturity that are worth holding on to, such as his theory of play and the in-between nature of it. The more problematic parts of his theory of maturity are found in the final chapter of his book, in which he describes the adolescent and the necessary growth beyond certain aspects of the teen years. Winnicott describes this in a way that we should leave behind, for we should not accept a version of maturity that encourages us to accept society and its demands as it is.

OF ADOLESCENTS, IDEALISTS, AND OTHERS

Freud makes clear in *The Interpretation of Dreams* that we should hold no romanticism regarding the psyches of children. Some theorists (like Rousseau) believe that humans are born naturally good and that society corrupts them. Freud, on the other hand, thinks that humans are born amoral and selfish and that parental and social training helps create a fully formed person who might become moral (as defined by that society). Therefore, no children are naturally good. He writes, "It is not difficult to see that the character even of a well-behaved child is not the character we should wish to find in an adult."[54] Furthermore, "A child is absolutely egotistical."[55]

Freud may be saying that children are morally neutral until socialized otherwise, but it seems that another interpretation is possible. One could read this to mean that all humans are born morally bad. By this reading, Freud is just as essentialist at Rousseau. One argues that human nature is essentially moral or inherently good, and the other argues that human nature is essentially immoral or inherently bad (until taught otherwise). In general, maybe it is true that children are selfish, although there are certainly examples of children doing selfless, altruistic things, typically based upon a kind of empathy or emotional appeal. I prefer a reading of Freud that is socially constructive rather than essentialist about human nature.

The Freudian path from selfish child to other-aware adult cannot be a smooth path. Of adolescence, Winnicott writes, "You can expect troubles."[56] If childhood "contained death," then adolescence "contained murder," since taking the parents' place and beginning to think for yourself is inherently aggressive.[57] Winnicott believes that adolescents are immature and that the adults around them must believe in their *own* maturity like never before, not allowing teens to believe in their own completed maturity. However, Winnicott also asserts that there are a precious few years of teen idealism during which the mind begins to understand the complexity of the world, and yet there is (usually) no responsibility for having to fully deal with this complexity. Winnicott deems this a "sacred element" of life.[58]

Let us analyze this idea of teens having "no individual responsibility for the world" and playfully link it to communism for a moment. Let us explore the idea that adolescents might be rebelling against the notion that to be an adult means to care only about oneself, one's family, one's status. After all, they have a front row seat to their parents'/guardians' attempts at "maturity" and they might recognize the utter sham of it all. Let us make a speculative claim: Communists can thus be compared to teenagers, in the best sense. We retain the idealistic vision that we can be freethinking, complex-thinking, pleasure-seeking, and at the same time not responsible for "adulting" for ourselves by ourselves. Capitalism seen through a liberalist philosophical belief in the individual has taught us this.

In his book *Liberalism and Democracy,* Italian philosopher Norberto Bobbio explains how the newer forms of liberalism (neoliberalism) became primarily an economic theory, not a political theory. That is, neoliberalism is first and foremost about the free market, and therefore individuals are "free" in relation to the negative liberty to not be restrained in their economic goals. (Obviously, liberals are not concerned with positive liberty; otherwise, they would be led to more socialist notions of the real possibility of engaging in economic activity.) "For Hayek, individual liberty, of which the first condition is economic freedom, possesses intrinsic value."[59] Liberalism is not, therefore, concerned with a good or healthy society, or good or healthy individuals. The goal is that no one shall impede another's free market activities.

Under the theory of liberalism, an adult is someone who engages fully in economic activity, someone who has money and spends it as they please. A child has no money of their own and thus cannot engage with the free market; they depend upon others for their economic/material sustenance. Thus far, liberals would probably not disagree with our linking of teens and communists, but as a matter of perspective, they would see this as a reason to dislike communism—i.e., it makes us "dependent" on others, the state becomes like our parents, whereas one ought to "grow up" and learn to support oneself materially. Such language is prevalent in our contemporary world: dependence is bad, autonomy is good. A capitalist society encourages us to believe that we can name and recognize our desires and that such desires can be fulfilled by market exchanges:

> We are all too familiar now with the idea that accurate recognition of ourselves and others is both possible and good for us; that we are able to acknowledge our needs and find out whether we have the capacity to meet them. Indeed consumer capitalism educates us in the virtues and easy pleasures of knowing ourselves and knowing what we want (knowing ourselves meaning simply knowing what we want to have). In this story, self-knowledge is the precondition for satisfaction.[60]

But what if we do not have clear self-knowledge?

It is a widespread belief that maturity means knowing who you are and what you want, that the self is a unified and known whole. Immaturity, then, must be precisely the opposite, a time when you have not yet figured out what you like or what satisfies you. Supposedly, we will discover what we lack and fill that lack. But most "adults" have only fashioned the appearance of having figured it out, and the lack and anxiety never really go away. Jacques Lacan helps us to understand this in his "mirror stage" piece.[61] At some point, we see a complete image of our body in a mirror and that image gives us a notion of completeness, self-sufficiency, autonomy. Inside, we know that we depend upon others, that we are fragmented, that we have conflicting desires, that we are decidedly *not whole*. But when we look in the mirror, we see a whole being. Thus begins our lifelong fantasy of believing that the thing in the mirror can be mature in a unified whole. It could be that social media has furthered this image creation. We create an image of ourselves online, and the thing we created seems more stable, better-looking, and altogether more "mature" than we know ourselves to be.

Herbert Marcuse talks about the humanist tradition as it relates to the development of students. The "humanities" as a field of studies used to be employed as a maturing tool, a set of texts and methodologies to teach young men how to be civilized and adult, how to be respectful of traditions and canons. It was also a colonialist tool for teaching the "savage" how to act like a bourgeois Christian White man. In 1962, Marcuse said that during the preceding 30 years, we learned "what human beings can be made to do"—they can be made to do inhumane things "in a pleasant enough way, so pliable and adaptable, that they can no longer defend themselves, so that are no longer capable of distinguishing truth from lies, education from propaganda."[62] Therefore, "we must relearn how to see, we must relearn how to think."[63] Marcuse shows us how civilization—projects of maturity—can lead in terrible directions. People can trick themselves (at some level) and others into believing that they are whole, unified, and educated, but be monsters.

LOVE, FRUSTRATION, AND "NOT GETTING IT"

For social movements and a robust politics, for friendship, and even for understanding science and the fallibility of all ideas, we need a community of open subjects interdependent on one another. This is at odds with the view of the self as autonomous and unified. We need subjects who are porous to the otherness of the world, who can think and love beyond self-preservation. Freud ultimately sees all love as an expansion of self: I only love others because I first love myself. All love builds outward from the subject: me, my mother, my family, my wider family, my neighborhood, my nation, etc. Freud believes that at its root, all love is narcissistic, and learning to love others begins from self-love and self-preservation (anaclitic love). If this is true, then love originates before, aside from, and without a totalizing understanding. Given that I am never a unified whole, I do not really understand myself, and yet I love myself, which means that I am at least capable of loving a confused object, *capable of loving while not grasping.*

Adam Phillips writes that we are keenly aware of our lack and "we are haunted by the myth of our own potential."[64] We say in modern culture that everyone should live up to their potential, be all they can be. But do we even know *what* we lack? Most marketing campaigns of universities build on this idea of unlocking students' potential. Many ethical systems judge a society on how well or how poorly it allows for the potential of its citizens to flourish (Aristotelians like Martha Nussbaum and Michael Sandel come to mind). Growth is expected in this potentiality "myth," as Phillips calls it.[65] We rarely speak of scarcity; rather, the dream is unending growth for everyone everywhere.

If we follow Freud that growing up is a process of gauging our own desires in comparison with what we can get out of the world, then the issue of scarcity is an important one. If we live with the idea that pleasure and the fulfillment of needs is limited (i.e., not everyone will be able to fulfill their desires), we enter our grown-up life in a battle against other people. Every person is potentially someone who might take pleasures away from me, so my life becomes a game of trying to get my slice of pie and maybe theirs, too. But Marcuse is correct that the culture around us shapes how we see scarcity. It is not an empirical fact for us when we enter the game. If you look at something like college entrance, this seems to reflect a reality that many live with: *Your* son getting into Oxford means one less chance for *my* son to get into Oxford. In fact, contemporary capitalism furthers this competition mindset—we even rank colleges and universities within the U.S. according to how many students they turn away.

What Marcuse does with this Freudian scheme is to say that if culture can amp up the belief in scarcity, we can get individuals to accept less. We can convince people to be happy ("grateful") for what they have. The world is dog-eat-dog, so feel lucky to have anything at all. We live in a constant fog of fear that there will not be enough for us. Hustle culture valorizes working harder because other people want what little I have. Other people are the enemy, they keep me from pleasure. If success is making money (which is how pleasure is defined in late capitalism), then the person who "succeeds" in this system is the one who is most suspicious of other people.

Part of what Winnicott means when he describes maturity as accepting the world for what it is seems to be the attitude of resignation—we resign ourselves to the world. At first glance, this seems sad. How can we retain the idealistic spark of an adolescent, a righteous anger that the world should be better than it is, and yet accept that we will not feel whole, we will not fully understand ourselves or our desires, and we will continually be interdependent with others? Part of the answer is in rejecting the easy answers. Our parents teach us that we are special, and modern capitalist culture persuades us that buying the right consumer products will ensure that we are special, but we know this is not true. Phillips puts it clearly: "first, ideally, we are made to feel special; then we are expected to enjoy a world in which we are not."[66] How can we be expected to care about others and about the world if we are not special? Or is it the reverse: Are we fascinated by the world and others precisely because we are not special?

Phillips makes a very Levinasian statement when he says that "people become real to us by frustrating us; if they don't frustrate us they are merely figures of fantasy."[67] If they frustrate us too much, then the persecution is too real and we harm them. If they frustrate us too little, then they are idealized and they become imaginary people in our minds. It is not quantifiable, but if it were, we "would say that the good life proposed by psychoanalysis is one in which there is just the right amount of frustration."[68] How might we accept frustration? How might we become suspicious of living a life of satisfaction, a life of believing that we understand ourselves and others, a life of what Phillips calls "getting it"? How might we avoid the tyranny of wanting to be around only the people, objects, art, and life situations that we "get"? As Phillips says, this means that the things around me fit into my fantasy without tension, but as most theorists of ethics will tell us, thinking about ethics and justice is precisely the opposite of that comfort. The word "scruples" gives us that sense—to be ethical is like having a small stone in your shoe. However, this is not a fully comprehended meaning (for either Levinas or Phillips). What if we could have a meaning whose meaning we do not fully get? That is desire to Lacan. And that is the power of the other to Levinas.

How might we learn to be comfortable with discomfort? Is it something we could teach, something we could help others develop in themselves? What kinds of practices could we engage in to help raise children who would be more at home with what Phillips calls "not getting it" and with what Levinas says is required for ethics: welcoming the other, as others have an effect on me that unsettles me. "The will to understand" seems to be our "second nature," according to Phillips.[69] How might we move beyond such a nature? When we are infants and children, we are in a state of pleasure and do not fully understand the world around us, the adult world. What Phillips wants us to consider is "what might precede getting it and not getting it"[70] and how we might become more at home with escaping that binary choice of getting it or not.

This dovetails nicely with our earlier comments about consumer capitalism. We are led to believe that we can know who we are and what we want. We are taught that we should expect to "get it" at every turn. If we do not get it, then we are not buying the right products or we are failures as individuals. Phillips asks, "why is it so difficult to enjoy not getting it?"[71] Part of the answer seems to be that our culture tells us that we should be getting it when we are keenly aware that we do not. A different set of social expectations, a different political reality, a different mode of "civilization" would encourage subjects to be sincere and open in recognizing their un-unified self as well as connecting to other un-unified selves. We are interested in promoting a subjectivity directed toward maturing that is not too fearful of the unknown, the unusual, the other—in short, the fear of something not fitting into your understanding (and your capacity for understanding) as it is now. How might we make that a willing development, a curiosity that is not grasping? How might I be curious in a way that does not pull the other into my sameness or reduce them to a piece in my synthesis, to allow non-knowing without allowing not knowing to become an excuse for not searching, a bad faith that allows ignorance to be an excuse for oppression and injustice? Not getting it cannot be an excuse for willful ignorance. We have duties to know how, when, where, and why our existence harms others, as Levinas says, how I may be taking someone else's "place in the sun" even though I do not intend to do so.

Jacqueline Rose writes that "there is no clear or easy resting place in the mind," that "fluidity, plasticity" are endemic to the subject.[72] Rather than arguing that we *ought* to be fluid in our desires and identities, Rose argues that we simply *are.* Coherence and stability are not ours. Thus, in Rose's view, it is by being honest to our experiences of subjectivity that we open ourselves to the "radical potential" of psychoanalysis. Each of us must ask: "Which is the more powerful? Our revolt against the world's inhumanity, or our tenacity in holding onto the identities" that we have constructed?[73] In a similar vein of arguing that psychoanalysis can help us frame our confused subjectivity, Michael Snediker, drawing on the work of both Winnicott and Eve Kosofsky Sedgwick, argues for an ethics of clearing a path for "not knowing in advance."[74] A psychoanalyst does this in the clinical setting, but it is also something that we all must do once we understand that a subject is never a done, stable, finished thing. No person is in a state of "is," no one is a "fact." While for Lacan, being ethical may be nothing more than following social norms, for Winnicott, being ethical requires that we leave a clearing for surprise, for conundra."[75]

In *Beyond Good and Evil*, Friedrich Nietzsche outlines three levels of morality that a society moves through: pre-moral, moral, and beyond-moral. At the highest level, mankind understands that what really pushes our actions and beliefs are unconscious drives and frustrations. We do not really know why we act the way we do. What is knowable to us, Nietzsche says, is like a skin: It reveals something, but it conceals more than it reveals.[76] It makes some sense if we read Nietzsche to say that the maturing of the individual and of a society requires approaching a progressively deeper and more complex understanding of ourselves. In that vein, Nietzsche seems to be saying that as we mature, we recognize how little we know or can know. Maturing should compel a curiosity that knows in advance that our probing minds surely will not figure it all out.

NOTES

1. Jacqueline Rose, "Something Amiss," in *Clinical Encounters in Sexuality: Psychoanalytic Practice and Queer Theory*, ed. Noreen Giffney and Eve Watson (Earth, Milky Way: Punctum Books, 2017), 391. Quoted with permission of Jacqueline Rose.

2. Donald Woods Winnicott, *Playing and Reality* (New York: Routledge Classics, 2005), 192–93.

3. Scott Graybow, *Progressive Psychoanalysis as a Social Justice Movement* (Newcastle upon Tyne, UK: Cambridge Scholars Publishing, 2017), 8.

4. Neil Altman, *Psychoanalysis in an Age of Accelerating Cultural Change: Spiritual Globalization* (New York: Routledge, 2015), quoted in Scott Graybow, *Progressive Psychoanalysis as a Social Justice Movement* (Newcastle upon Tyne, UK: Cambridge Scholars Publishing, 2017), 8.

5. Sigmund Freud, *Civilization and Its Discontents*, trans. and ed. James Strachey (New York: W.W. Norton), 16–19.

6. Freud, *Civilization and Its Discontents*, 13.

7. Freud, *Civilization and Its Discontents*, 13–14.

8. Freud, *Civilization and Its Discontents*, 15.

9. Freud, *Civilization and Its Discontents*, 15.

10. Julia Kristeva, *Intimate Revolt: The Powers and Limits of Psychoanalysis*, trans. Jeanine Herman (New York: Columbia University Press, 2002), 234.

11. Freud, *Civilization and Its Discontents*, 12.

12. Freud, *Civilization and Its Discontents*, 13.

13. Freud, *Civilization and Its Discontents*, 13.

14. Sigmund Freud, "Three Contributions to the Theory of Sex," in *The Basic Writings of Sigmund Freud,* trans. and ed. A.A. Brill (New York: The Modern Library, 1995), 521.

15. Freud, "Three Contributions to the Theory of Sex," 528.

16. Freud, "Three Contributions to the Theory of Sex," 574.

17. Freud, "Three Contributions to the Theory of Sex," 574.

18. Freud, "Three Contributions to the Theory of Sex," 522–30.

19. Freud, "Three Contributions to the Theory of Sex," 580.

20. Freud, "Three Contributions to the Theory of Sex," 581.

21. Freud, "Three Contributions to the Theory of Sex," 583.

22. Etienne Balibar, *Citizen Subject: Foundations of Philosophical Anthropology* (New York: Fordham University Press, 2017), 294.

23. Balibar, *Citizen Subject*, 294.

24. Ann Murphy, "The Redress of Psychoanalysis," in *Clinical Encounters in Sexuality: Psychoanalytic Practice and Queer Theory*, ed. Noreen Giffney and Eve Watson (Earth, Milky Way: Punctum Books, 2017), 224.

25. Murphy, "The Redress of Psychoanalysis," 225.

26. Murphy, "The Redress of Psychoanalysis," 226.

27. Winnicott, *Playing and Reality*, 141.

28. Winnicott, *Playing and Reality*, 7.

29. Winnicott, *Playing and Reality*, 16.

30. Winnicott, *Playing and Reality*, 17.

31. Winnicott, *Playing and Reality*, 18.

32. Winnicott, *Playing and Reality,* 192–93.

33. Winnicott, *Playing and Reality*, 24–26.

34. Winnicott, *Playing and Reality*, 51.

35. Winnicott, *Playing and Reality*, 72.

36. Winnicott, *Playing and Reality*, 99.

37. Winnicott, *Playing and Reality*, 51, 74–76.

38. Winnicott, *Playing and Reality*, 76.

39. Winnicott, *Playing and Reality*, 116.
40. Winnicott, *Playing and Reality*, 116.
41. Winnicott, *Playing and Reality*, 87.
42. Winnicott, *Playing and Reality*, 87–88.
43. Maurice Merleau-Ponty, *Phenomenology of Perception*, trans. Donald A. Landes (New York: Routledge, 2012).
44. Winnicott, *Playing and Reality,* 129.
45. Winnicott, *Playing and Reality*, 121.
46. Brown, Norman O. Life Against Death: The Psychoanalytical Meaning of History (Middletown: Wesleyan University Press, 1959), 6.
47. Winnicott, *Playing and Reality*, 133–34.
48. Winnicott, *Playing and Reality,* 157–58.
49. Winnicott, *Playing and Reality*, 161.
50. Winnicott, *Playing and Reality*, 186–87.
51. Martha C. Nussbaum, *Frontiers of Justice: Disability, Nationality, Species Membership* (Cambridge, MA: Harvard University Press, 2009), 413.
52. Karl Marx, "Estranged Labor," in *Economic and Philosophic Manuscripts of 1844*, https://www.marxists.org/archive/marx/works/1844/manuscripts/labour.htm.
53. Winnicott, *Playing and Reality*, 188.
54. Sigmund Freud, *The Interpretation of Dreams*, trans. A.A. Brill (Hertfordshire, UK: Wordsworth Editions Limited, 1997), 267.
55. Freud, *The Interpretation of Dreams,* 267.
56. Winnicott, *Playing and Reality*, 195.
57. Winnicott, *Playing and Reality*, 195–96.
58. Winnicott, *Playing and Reality*, 198.
59. Norberto Bobbio, *Liberalism and Democracy* (New York: Verso Books, 2005), 81.
60. Adam Phillips, *Missing Out: In Praise of the Unlived Life* (New York: Farrar, Straus and Giroux, 2013), 36.
61. Jacques Lacan, "The Mirror Stage as Formative of the *I* Function as Revealed in Psychoanalytic Experience," in *Écrits: The First Complete Edition in English*, trans. Bruce Fink (New York: W.W. Norton and Company, 2006), 75–81.
62. Herbert Marcuse, *Marxism, Revolution and Utopia: Collected Papers of Herbert Marcuse, Volume 6*, eds. Douglas Kellner and Clayton Pierce (New York: Routledge, 2014), 106.
63. Marcuse, *Marxism, Revolution and Utopia*, 106.
64. Phillips, *Missing Out*, xii–xiii.
65. Phillips, *Missing Out*, xiv.
66. Phillips, *Missing Out*, xv.
67. Phillips, *Missing Out*, 29.
68. Phillips, *Missing Out*, 30.
69. Phillips, *Missing Out*, 56.
70. Phillips, *Missing Out*, 37.
71. Phillips, *Missing Out*, 45.
72. Rose, "Something Amiss," 391.

73. Rose, "Something Amiss," 394.

74. Michael Snediker, "Out of Line, On Hold: D.W. Winnicott's Queer Sensibilities," in *Clinical Encounters in Sexuality: Psychoanalytic Practice and Queer Theory*, ed. Noreen Giffney and Eve Watson (Earth, Milky Way: Punctum Books, 2017), 146.

75. Snediker, "Out of Line, On Hold," 151.

76. Friedrich Nietzsche, *Beyond Good and Evil: Prelude to a Philosophy of the Future*, trans. and commentary by Walter Kaufmann (New York: Vintage Books, 1989), 44.

Chapter Three

Failure and Immaturity

". . . free from seriousness and the boredom of maturity."

—Maurice Blanchot[1]

It seems as if Herbert Marcuse and Norman O. Brown take the perspective of the id (all is unity, oceanic, Eros, play) and philosophy in general takes the perspective of the ego (all is rational, separable, and analyzable). But is it not Freud's point that *both* perspectives (in concert with the superego) are right, that this contradiction of desires is what constitutes the person who has an archaeology of three levels that may not always agree on the what, why, or how of desire? What the id wants, the ego puts into the context of "real" social constraints, and the superego warns against it. It is not that one level should master the others (as Marcuse and Brown seem to want) but that all three levels exist in the person, who must find a way of negotiating the world while being increasingly complex and open to it.

The ideas of Maurice Blanchot are helpful here, as he explains two levels of thought, one that operates in a rational, Hegelian way and another that operates in an irrational, more Nietzschean way. He outlines these two levels in particular with regards to death. There is a way of understanding death that is rational, as the ending of life, as a stopping point and finitude that gives meaning to our lives. The second, irrational way of understanding death is precisely the lack of finitude, a death from which we gain no meaning or power. Blanchot is helpful in understanding the development of the person amid contradiction because, like Freud, he describes contradictory levels within the subject. Blanchot finds no need to combine the levels into wholeness, to eradicate contradiction. Rather, a subject lives in the midst of contradiction, uses the power of the dialectic to understand parts of the world such as, for instance, practical politics, where the materialist Hegelian dialectic ought to be helpful. But a subject must also deal with the darker, more irrational side, recognizing and trying to grasp and wrestle with it. For Blanchot, it is this darker side that provides energy for art.

There exists a certain parallel in Nietzsche's division between the Apollonian and Dionysian forces. Indeed, Brown emphasizes that we need to return to the Dionysian, to the full power of Eros. Again, Blanchot offers a helpful solution and clarification. It is not that we must pick a side, Apollonian or Dionysian; rather, a subject must learn to accept both and live in the midst of the contradiction it necessarily entails. This also resonates with Freud, whose archaeological approach makes it clear that all three levels exist in the adult. One could no more erase the superego and return to the id than one could entirely wipe out the id and live on the power of the superego. For me, then, Brown and Marcuse have misunderstood Freud. They have chosen one layer of the archeology and raised it above the others. Perhaps their move is merely dialectical, as the id has been given short shrift in our late capitalist, performance-principle era. I agree with both of them that we need more focus on the pleasure principle and pure play. But *more* is not *all*. There is no pure return to id, according to Freud, nor should there be.

Here is where I think Brown goes further (in an adverse way) than Marcuse. Brown believes that we should fully return to the pleasure of the id, remove all boundaries, remove all rationality of the reality principle, and embrace Eros. He even suggests that we will not get rid of strife and war until we get rid of all separation into individual selves, for "to have a self is to have enemies, and to be a self is to be at war. . . to abolish war, therefore, is to abolish the self: and the war to end war is total war; to have no more enemies or self."[2] Like Nancy Chodorow, I disagree. Brown has no community and he has no political ethics. Both require a robust understanding of the *otherness of the other*. Getting rid of all boundaries, subsuming the other into my own narcissism, will not respect her otherness and difference. Chodorow writes,

> We become a person, then, in internal relation with the social world. This social world, even at its worst, is not purely constraining, as Brown and Marcuse would have it. . . nor could it ever completely eliminate the individual. People inevitably incorporate one another; our sociality is built into our psychic structure and there is no easy separation of individual and society or possibility of the individual apart from society.[3]

Like Chodorow, I believe that human subjects (not precluding other species) can never get completely rid of the individual or of the social. Both are integral to what a subject is. Therefore, to understand maturing, we need a multi-level, interdependent conception of the human person.

Blanchot, in *The Space of Literature,* describes two possible ways of thinking about death. On the one hand, we can think of our own death as the impetus for our activity and ambition in life; because I recognize my finitude, I have projects and goals in life. Just as sleeping at night gives one the ability and power to live during the day, being aware of one's finitude can be the start of living purposely, actively. This is death as possibility. On the other hand, we can think of our own death as an incomprehensible abyss, an irrational death from which we can gain no use, no power, no relation. Nothing productive or dialectical stems from this second mode of death: "the time of time's absence is not dialectical."[4] This is death as impossibility. In his reading of Kafka, Blanchot finds two deaths, insincere and sincere, that correspond to the death as possibility and impossibility, respectively. Kafka rather arrogantly says regarding his own death that, unlike other men, he will be able to die satisfied and pleased with himself: "I keep a much clearer head than he, who will lament, I suppose, on his deathbed."[5] Blanchot, always suspicious of bravado, asserts that it is "precisely because of his [Kafka's] irritating insincerity" that his outlook here is "revealing," as Kafka brags about his own "mastery" as "power through and through."[6] Kafka's "contentment is then very close to Hegelian wisdom" since "in extreme negativity" death becomes "possibility, project, and time."[7] It is in this way that an artist or any person with ambition seeks to glorify themselves through their projects, to make their lives meaningful through action against the negative in order to be able to look back on their lives with pride about the way they lived and what they accomplished. There is self-satisfaction, the idea that self-satisfaction is even possible or desirable. It sounds like a very macho death, even in the hands of Kafka. (Machismo is like that, meant to pressure all men to prove their strength and manhood.) In this way, death is to be *achieved,* for it is the "source of our activity and mastery." Put succinctly, "Man dies, that is nothing. But man is, starting from his death."[8] In this case, I think Blanchot's use of "man" (*homme*) to refer to all of humanity seems suitable.

The problem is that this is too clear, too rational for what death is; to understand death as merely useful and productive is to not fully deal with death, and "the essential escapes us."[9] Indeed, "A death that is free, useful, and conscious, that is agreeable to the living, in which the dying person remains true to himself, is a death that has not met with death."[10] This other death is impersonal and gives us no power. Blanchot writes,

> . . . death is somehow doubled: there is one death which circulates in the language of possibility, of liberty, which has for its furthest horizon the freedom to die and the capacity to take mortal risks; and there is its double, which is ungraspable. It is what I cannot grasp, what is not linked to *me* by any relation of any sort. It is that which never comes and toward which I do not direct myself.[11]

The ideas Blanchot uses to describe this impossible death are failure, incompletion, anonymity, uselessness. Sometimes he calls this the "other night," the "deeper night," or "midnight." Midnight is "pure presence where nothing but the subsistence of nothing subsists" and "neutrality and impersonality in which nothing is accomplished."[12] It is not an "I die" but a "They die," since this has no link to the particularity or authenticity of me. With this impossible death, we are introduced to absolute otherness and alterity with which we can have no relation.

Blanchot links this impossible side of death to art and the space of literature. In literature's space, there is no utility; utilitarian projects fall apart because there is no mastery, no "tools."[13] People often say that artists have found a way to withdraw "from life's responsibilities" in order to "protect" themselves "from the world where action is difficult"[14] or that artists are weak creatures who cannot deal with reality. Perhaps, but why is weakness in the face of the world not a philosophically correct position? From Blanchot's perspective, the artist is the brave one who "willingly exposes himself to the risks" of uncertainty and to a space where "he does not feel that he is master of himself."[15] From that perspective, the world is a refuge from the space of art, not the other way around. Here we see Blanchot deeming the weakness of the artist a strength: "a new strength is born in them at the very point where they succumb to the extremity of their weakness."[16]

Emmanuel Levinas, in *Existence and Existents,* references Blanchot's work in helping him formulate the idea of the "there is" (the *il y a*). The "there is" is an anonymous, impersonal force with which we can have no dialectical relation, from which we can learn nothing and build nothing. If this all seems a bit too abstract, Levinas asks us to "imagine all beings, things and persons, reverting to nothingness," to imagine "the night and silence of nothingness."[17] Some people have a glimmer of this sense of nothingness when they think about the vastness of the universe in time and space in comparison to our own subjective perception of time and space. According to Levinas, the "there is" is the "dark background of existence" where there is "no determined being, anything can count for anything else."[18] A helpful metaphor here is sleep as the power that drives our daytime wakefulness—sleep as a part of our subjectivity, our power to be subjects. However, insomnia is closer to the absence of subjectivity. "The possibility of resting, of being closed up in oneself, is the possibility of giving oneself over to the base, of going to bed" whereas, in insomnia, "Wakefulness is anonymous" and it is "not that there is *my* vigilance in the night; in insomnia it is the night itself that watches. It watches" and the "ego is swept away."[19] As with Blanchot, we have two levels of relatedness to the world, one that is dialectical, including positive and negative in a play of growth and possibility, and another that is the absence of subjectivity and power.

With regards to the work of making art, the writer never feels entirely in control of the process for Blanchot: "he never knows when the work is done" and the "writer only finishes his work at the moment he dies."[20] We could read this in relation to the work of creating the self, too. We do not know if we are done and we do not have control over the process. It is "neither finished nor unfinished; it is."[21] Blanchot also emphasizes that mastery is putting the pencil aside, stopping the writing rather than picking it up. He inspires us to rethink our interactions with the world in terms of activity and passivity. If we compare the writer's mastery to the mastery we have over our maturing, we conclude that we have mastery to the degree that we recognize that we are not fully in control, not fully authentic, that others influence us, are always already a part of us, mark us. We must stop trying to have total mastery of the self, stop believing that the self can "bootstrap" itself into existence, and contemplate this relation with the other and with the otherness of the world. We begin to have some "mastery" over our maturing when we stop trying so obsessively to mature by focusing on the power of the self. This is "the ungraspable in action."[22]

In a similar vein, I would suggest that the more mature we become, the more uncertain we become about that maturity, including our goals and projects in the world. As Blanchot says of Kafka, the more that Kafka writes, "the less sure he is of writing."[23] As we mature, our conceptual tools ought to grow more complex. How we understand our present reality ought to broaden; moreover, our past experiences can be understood in a very different way. Our own childhoods often fascinate us because, at the time, we did not know how to give them sense.[24] The process of analysis is a tool in beginning to reconceptualize our experiences and how we have matured. We can begin to see with a newer, hopefully wiser perception, by which I mean the growing ability to conceptualize at multiple levels of complexity.

BLANCHOT ON FAILURE

When the subject stops becoming a project of total power and ability, and when we give ourselves over to otherness, we can find what Blanchot refers to as "the becoming of interruption," which we become only through the interruption of others and in motion with others.[25] Blanchot always insists on the otherness and strangeness of the other; it is an ethical obligation not to reduce other experiences or people to our own categories and our own projects. Of this ethical relation, he introduces the concept of the *interval*: "What separates becomes relation" and this requires an interval, "the pure interval that, from me to this other who is a friend, measures all that is between us, the interruption of being."[26] Far from preventing communication, this interval is understood as what allows the very possibility of it.

In a rare moment of a short sentence with a clear meaning, Blanchot writes, "Success simplifies."[27] The verifiable, assessable world that gives you success deludes you into believing and living too much in that world. This is another reason why we should never confuse maturity with success in the world. Successful people in our present world are generally more narrow-minded and self-absorbed, given the personalities and behaviors that capitalism rewards. And once people achieve "success," they often become too sure of themselves and stop asking questions; they stop listening for difference. Everything can become abstract cliché. From my own experience at a university attending meetings of both the high and low in the hierarchy, it has always seemed to me that the service workers (custodians, painters, electricians) are generally broader thinkers, more attuned to the specificity of the world and to the experiences of others, than are the top administration and board. All too often, those at the top of the hierarchy refrain from asking meaningful questions or grasping complexities. They all too easily believe in the systems that got them where they are. This is in alignment with Blanchot's claim that "Success simplifies." The modern successful man spends all his efforts toward "Possessions, honors, all that attaches him to reality" since this "helps him make what he has made into a sure, complete, verifiable world."[28] The successful man must push away conscience and curiosity, "keeping himself close to himself" since he knows the "destructive power of conscience," and, above all, keep himself from "tormenting curiosity."[29] He exists in the realm of a language of "domination and energy" and not of curiosity, chance, or ambiguity, which we need to exist in a realm of "infinite demand."[30] At some level, we all know that life is confusing, absurd, lacking in coherent meaning. Some have not learned how to live with that contradiction in ways other than repressing it and chasing success and approval in the way our culture offers it. Reversion to simple falsehoods is a sure sign of immaturity.

What Blanchot says of the work of literature, we might suggest of life itself: It must have "possibility at its center."[31] The problem with the normative conception of the adult is that possibility and experimentation has been lost, given up, abandoned. Blanchot writes that "the true man is more important than the angel, because the angel stands immobile" whereas man is in "the process of becoming" and "not through himself alone."[32]

Blanchot engages directly with phenomenology when he addresses consciousness and our relatedness to the world. He writes that we are beings often freed from the here and now thanks to consciousness. While always woven together in and with the external world, we turn away from the world in order to grasp it, to move "toward higher or more demanding meanings."[33]

This may seem only tangentially related to the idea of maturity, but the workings of consciousness can never be far from the understanding of how we grow, how our consciousness might expand or withhold, connect or disconnect.

In June 2020, the United States experienced one of the largest protests in its history. In all 50 states and many other countries as well, there were protests against racism and police brutality in the wake of the murders of George Floyd, Breonna Taylor, Ahmaud Arbery, and others. Racism in the U.S. is not new, nor is it novel within the police—it goes back to the founding of the American police force itself, which was created to control enslaved Black people.[34] The numbers of people involved in protesting racism during the Black Lives Matter movement, however, are unprecedented. Because I have linked maturity and activism, it makes sense to look at the position of the protestor. I argue that there are two demands on the protestor that seem contradictory at first glance. On the one hand, a protestor must study (in this particular case) how racism structures institutions, schools, banking policies, neighborhoods, healthcare, the police, and so forth. In protesting, we demand that the structures of our society change. This demand requires that we focus our perception on the external world, that we take a closer and more critical look at it and demand that others also take up that perceptive lens.

On the other hand, there is the demand that a protestor must look inside herself and focus her perception on the internal world. We must look into our own consciousness, our own ideas and concepts, how we thought about or passively accepted the present state of affairs—in this case, of the police, prisons, or schools. What is my own experience with those institutions? Why and according to what grounds has that been my experience? This is deeply personal work, both psychological and philosophical. Blanchot argues that while it may appear that we go further inside the self in order to withdraw from the world, we do not. We do not go inside the self merely to escape the problems of the world but to see those problems more rigorously, to create inside of ourselves "higher and more demanding meanings."[35] In fact, without this movement of individuals going inside themselves, activists will make many mistakes and might ultimately derail a cause. This is a big discussion in activist circles at the moment, and rightly so. We build a movement for change by changing the systems and structures in the world, and that work must be done collaboratively, by and for the people. At the same time, changing systems means also changing ourselves, not clinging to ideas we held years ago, even yesterday, but maturing past those ideas. This means ruffling what we thought was already understood in our consciousness. The danger in believing that "I already understand all that" seems to be more difficult to move past the older we get, for the normative idea of maturity is that when we have more years under our belts, we necessarily understand more and stand on solid ground. This is one reason why properly understanding maturing is vital to creating better political systems. Blanchot never lets us have stability or rest in our consciousness. Anarchy of the consciousness is always possible, and that is a good thing. To be fully rational and knowing is dangerous—it is the self-satisfaction of the fascist.

QUEER THEORY ON IMMATURITY AND FAILURE

Queer theory includes at least one division of thought related to Blanchot's division of thought, a division also related to the concepts of failure and success. Shall we favor a pure negation (per Lee Edelman) or shall we opt for a negation that would ultimately be politically useful and idealistic (per José Esteban Muñoz)? I think it is helpful to understand this division within queer theory because both sides reference psychoanalytic theory and seek a way of escaping the power of the normalizing culture toward the queer. *What is "queer"?* is at the heart of this issue. To some (like Edelman), queerness is a retreat, a refusal to participate in the forward-thinking, developmental, adult narrative of heteronormative life. To others, like Muñoz, to be queer is a project for the future: We are always trying to be queer, developing and evolving toward the queer. Muñoz's future resonates with Derrida's sense of the "to come"—future-oriented hope, never bound to essences or presence. So, on the one hand is a negation that refuses to play the political game, on the other hand is a negation that critiques the present in the name of the future. Blanchot's double negation is helpful here once again. Let us keep both meanings of queer and both meanings of negation in mind as we think through *immaturity as failure.*

Let us look briefly at Edelman's work. He takes up the image of The Child in the Lacanian way. Just as, for Lacan, the "phallus" is not the same thing as the penis, The Child is not the same thing as *a* child. The Child is more of a symbol of the way that heteronormative culture lives. It represents putting all our faith in the future and its reproduction. In this model, you become an adult to the degree that you play your part in futurism. You are either a child or you should be raising a child. Maturity, then, is acquiescence to marriage and raising children. Queer is associated with revelry, rebellion, and remaining a "child" in the sense of escaping boring adult decrees. It is enough to make one drop the goal of "maturing" altogether.

In one of the funniest openings to a book that I have encountered, Edelman begins his book *No Future: Queer Theory and the Death Drive* by recounting a story about President Bill Clinton pandering to the Coalition for America's

Children because "public appeals on behalf of America's children" have a social consensus that is "impossible to refuse."[36] Edelman quips, "We're fighting for the children. Whose side are you on?"[37] In our time, he writes, The Child is the "perpetual horizon of every acknowledged politics, the fantasmatic beneficiary of every political intervention."[38] But Edelman boldly asserts that within his own project, "*queerness* names the side of those *not* 'fighting for the children,'" outside the political demand of "reproductive futurism."[39] Edelman is clear that this is not a negation that does political work but is the absence and retreat from politics. His ironic humor comes at a cost! Queerness is a challenge to politics and to the social value itself. It refuses any "backdoor hope for dialectical access to meaning."[40] Edelman believes that The Child is the secular theology that our culture thrives on. As Edelman quotes Lauren Berlant, "a nation made for adult citizens has been replaced by one imagined for fetuses and children."[41] There is no inherent value in the present or in present people, for their value lies only in their having children and then those children having children, ad infinitum (or until the planet collapses). Edelman is right that reproductive futurity looks like a Ponzi scheme.

I do think that Edelman (perhaps unconsciously) hints sideways at a negativity that could be construed as political, even though consciously he adamantly denies this type of social-political negativity. Instead of queer, he more often uses the word "*sinthomo*sexuals," a concept that aligns with the death drive against futurity and sociality by a "constitutive fixation of the subject's access to jouissance" without any "fantasy of futurism."[42] The "*sinthomo*sexual won't offer a blessed thing by way of salvation, won't promise any transcendence or grant us a vision of something to come" and, in fact, "forsakes all causes, all social action, all responsibility for a better tomorrow."[43] A symbol that he uses to represent the undoing of meaning is the birds in Alfred Hitchcock's 1963 film *The Birds*. Edelman argues that the birds represent nonsensical, meaningless violence and can be related to the position of the *sinthomo*sexual.[44] The birds are apolitically violent; there is no ethical meaning to their attacks.

Yet, in the same book, Edelman asks us to recall the death of Matthew Shepard. It is in this section of his work where I believe we might uncover a sideways nod at the political, calling into question his claim of apolitical queerness. Shepard, a young gay man, was beaten, tortured, and left for dead near Laramie, Wyoming, on a cold night in 1998. In the wake of his murder, Shepard's mother told mourners to "go home and give your kids a hug tonight."[45] Edelman comments on "these words, which even on the occasion of a gay man's murder defined the proper mourners as those who had children to go home and hug."[46] Cannot those not invested in the politics of reproductive futurity mourn? Edelman is right to critique this, but where does his critique come from? How can we critique this utterance without a politics? If we "have no vision of something to come" and "forsake all causes," why care about who does or does not get to mourn the murder of Matthew Shepard? In the last lines of his book, Edelman writes, "Somewhere, someone else will be savagely beaten and left to die—sacrificed to a future whose beat goes on" and meanwhile, we continue focusing on leaving no child behind while murdering the *sinthomo*sexuals.[47] It is interesting that he ends the book on this note of sadness and rage, a rage that is proper but useless if one believes that queer people's positionality is to be only antisocial, anti-political symbols.

There is a certain way in which Edelman's ideas on immaturity resonate with those of Donald Winnicott. That is, becoming an adult means becoming stable, secure, pragmatic, responsible, boring, a cog in the wheel of reproducing the current culture into the future. (Of course, Winnicott and Edelman would disagree on the importance we should give The Child, although they might agree on certain aspects of bringing play into the adult world.) I appreciate Edelman's correction to our cultural emphasis—obsession, perhaps—on reproductive futurity. I agree with him that a corrective is needed. However, like Jack Halberstam, I think Edelman's sense of the negative is too apolitical and ironic. Maybe if one is a White, middle-class, gay man, one can afford to be ironic regarding political commitments (although the example of Matthew Shepard suggests otherwise), but for most of us, politics is life-and-death serious.

Halberstam argues that Edelman's apolitical negativity has no way of critiquing reproductive futurism because it merely says "yeah, we queers are not that" but leaves the ideology untouched. Halberstam writes in *The Queer Art of Failure* that, for Edelman, the "queer is always and inevitably linked to the death drive," opposed to the "heteronormative politics of hope."[48] Halberstam wants to take Edelman's basic insight of the "antisocial project" and "argue for a more political framing" and does so by referring to the punk movement and specifically to the Sex Pistols as an example of how to have an antisocial negative that is political. Instead of irony, punk has rage. Halberstam references the Sex Pistols' 1977 song "God Save the Queen" with the refrain "No future" to "reject a formulaic union of nation, monarchy and fantasy," "a rallying cry for Britain's dispossessed" and a "snarling rejection" of "the divisions of class and race upon which the notion of national belonging depends."[49] For Halberstam (and me), the Sex Pistols' negativity wins over Edelman's. And the reason? "Negativity might well constitute an antipolitics, but it should not register as apolitical."[50]

We see here the two types of negativity that Blanchot discussed, one that is dialectical and politically useful (first death) and the other that is not (second death). Edelman only includes the second type of negativity, the one not in relation to or with the world. Halberstam, like Blanchot, thinks we need both understandings of negativity. Sara Ahmed agrees with Edelman's critique of the normative "straight line" that exists among lesbians and gays, writing, "We are right to be critical of such a conservative sexual politics, which 'supports' the very lines that make some lives unlivable."[51] She believes that a kind of gay conservatism is alive and well. In this vein, she critiques a book within queer studies that, instead of Edelman's negative approach, takes a positive approach: Bruce Bawer's *A Place at the Table: The Gay Individual in American Society*. This positive approach is even worse by my (and, I think, Ahmed's) reckoning. Bawer claims that, instead of leading separate queer lives that negate normative values—what he calls sitting at the "little table" (i.e., with children)—gays ought to move to the "big table" with the adults, which would mean acquiescing to the normative beliefs and practices of those at that big table: be monogamous, get married, have children, etc. Bawer describes as adult precisely the things I am arguing against in this book. Regarding the gay man, Bawer states,

> He doesn't *want* to be assimilated. He enjoys his exclusion. He feels comfortable at his little table. Or at least he thinks he does. But does he? What is it, after all, that ties him to his little table—that drove him, in other words, into a marginal existence? Ultimately, it's prejudice. Liberated from that prejudice, would he still want to sit at his little table? Perhaps, and perhaps not. Certainly most homosexuals don't want to be relegated to that little table. We grew up at the big table: we're at home there. We want to stay there.[52]

Why should we necessarily want what is "at home"? For many people, "home" is not a good place, given conservative notions of the roles in the nuclear family (more about that in chapter 5). Bawer wrongly assumes that "at home" is something everyone either wants or will benefit from socially/psychologically, developmentally, or ethically. I would argue that no one should want it, at least in its present form. Bawer rejects queer subcultures and wants "a return to the family table."[53] As Ahmed rightly points out, the "big table" stands in for traditional family values and normative society itself; maturity, then, is about finally accepting the big table and its norms. Fortunately, Bawer's conservative positivity and Edelman's apolitical negativity are not our only options.

In my view, we need to use the force of the negative in critiquing normative society in order to mature, but how? Again, Halberstam is helpful in linking queerness to failure and to childhood: "Childhood, as many queers in particular recall, is a long lesson in humility, awkwardness, [and] limitation."[54] There is something queerly unruly about childhood since we all have to be *taught* how to be so-called adults. We are prodded to "become 'mature' through marriage" by "being pushed through a series of maturational models of growth."[55] But childhood also gives us hope, for that path to normative maturity is not a given, not natural or universal: "If we were all already normative and heterosexual to begin with in our desires, orientations, and modes of being, then presumably we would not need such strict parental guidance to deliver us all to our common destinies of marriage, child rearing, and hetero-reproduction."[56]

In "Theorizing Queer Temporalities: A Roundtable Discussion," Halberstam tells a personal narrative of being a child in England in the 1970s surrounded by teachers who pressured the students to follow the normative path ruled by masculine desire. The headmistress scolded young girls for the way they dressed, for provoking the sexual desires of male teachers. She instructed them that it is best to acquiesce to male rule early in life as it "will be good training for us as we prepare ourselves for marriage and family." Halberstam rejected it all: "I hear a loud voice in my head saying fuck family, fuck marriage, fuck the male teachers, this is not my life, that will not be my time line."[57] Instead, Halberstam chose a "way of being in the world and a critique of the careful social scripts that usher even the most queer among us through major markers of individual development and into normativity."[58]

On the other hand, in *The Trouble with Normal: Sex, Politics, and the Ethics of Queer Life,* Michael Warner critiques the LGBT movement as not queer enough. This has a relationship to our project because "normal" is considered to be "grown up" and Warner is opposed to it. He calls marriage "unethical" and slams the desire to "be normal." Or, in Halberstam's words, it comes across as a "plea for the right to become 'mature' through marriage."[59] Normal is an attempt at anti-political politics—blend in, no conflict, just wait for some "trickle-down acceptance."[60] *The Trouble with Normal* is in unapologetic praise of "queer," which Warner separates from LGBT. Queer society at first seems like revelry in everything, no rules, relative and libertine, but Warner is no relativist. He argues that there is an ethic in queer culture: "Get over yourself."[61] Sex is shameful and messy, and queer people know this and are able to find dignity in shame. This queer ethic forbids pinning your shame on someone else, as bigots usually do. Warner claims that "bourgeois propriety" gives dignity to married, private, loving sex; in queer culture, however, "there is no truck with bourgeois propriety."[62] In queer culture, our dignity is a shared indignity binding people together. Warner's sense of shame is easily linked to the praise of failure in Blanchot and Halberstam. The ethic of *get over yourself* is precisely what we need in order to be in the process of maturing.

We can link José Esteban Muñoz's idea of "becoming queer" to Blanchot's useful negativity because our bodies exist in the political present. We must politically commit to the world, but in such a way that we are open to unknown possibilities. According to Muñoz, queer is a goal always on the horizon, never a stable identity that one can claim to "have" or "be." I argue that queer needs to be more than absence, more than apolitical negativity. A passive retreat to the corner and "refusing to play the game" is not sufficient. Sometimes you need to walk up to the game in process and flip the damn table. An excellent example of this is the "terrorist" drag and "critical uneasiness" of performer Vaginal Creme Davis as discussed by Muñoz in *Disidentifications: Queers of Color and the Performance of Politics.* Davis started in the Los Angeles punk scene with bands like X. She is a drag queen who is Black and Mexican by birth, and the punk scene, especially early on, was for angry White boys. Davis enters this scene in double drag, in drag as a woman in drag as a White supremacist militiaman known as Clarence, and to quote Muñoz, "Clarence has as much of a chance to pass as White as Vaginal has to pass as female."[63] Here, disidentification works as critique; "passing" and "realness" are not the point. "Failure" works as critique of the norms of identity. Furthermore, Clarence, the name that Vaginal Davis chose for the White militiaman character? That is her actual birth name. The desire for authenticity is presented to us as *a joke.*

In aligning with Blanchot and Muñoz, we are in a position to recognize that two types of negativity are necessary in grappling with the types of questions that maturing raises. On the one hand, we can see that there is some type of Hegelian progression from our childhood onward. On the other hand, it is equally true to say that this progression is false, that what we often progress in are the normative values of our society. Believing in the "progress" of the individual in this way links one to the belief that the values of our society are politically ethical, that those values deserve our learning and adhering to them. That is not my position. I see wisdom in the work of Blanchot, who asks us to fail, to waste our time. I see wisdom in Halberstam asking us to fail and remain immature, to be childlike. I see wisdom in Muñoz extolling adolescent rebellion and outsider chaos. Failure, immaturity, and the critique of identity are ways of rejecting the clean path of maturity that society hands us, which was never really about maturing but was always about imposing social norms.

NOTES

1. Maurice Blanchot, *Friendship,* trans. Elizabeth Rottenberg (Stanford: Stanford University Press, 1997), 80. Quoted with permission of Stanford University Press.
2. Norman O. Brown, *Love's Body* (New York: Random House, 1966), 149.
3. Nancy J. Chodorow, *Feminism and Psychoanalytic Theory* (New Haven: Yale University Press, 1989), 149.

4. Maurice Blanchot, *The Space of Literature,* trans. Ann Smock (Lincoln: University of Nebraska Press, 1982), 30.
5. Blanchot, *The Space of Literature*, 90.
6. Blanchot, *The Space of Literature,* 91.
7. Blanchot, *The Space of Literature,* 91.
8. Blanchot, *The Space of Literature*, 96.
9. Blanchot, *The Space of Literature*, 101.
10. Blanchot, *The Space of Literature*, 101.
11. Blanchot, *The Space of Literature,* 104.
12. Blanchot, *The Space of Literature,* 112.
13. Blanchot, *The Space of Literature,* 51.
14. Blanchot, *The Space of Literature,* 52.
15. Blanchot, *The Space of Literature,* 53.
16. Blanchot, *The Space of Literature,* 55.
17. Emmanuel Levinas, *Existence and Existents,* trans. Alphonso Lingis (Dordrecht: Kluwer Academic Press, 1995), 57.
18. Levinas, *Existence and Existents*, 60, 59.
19. Levinas, *Existence and Existents*, 72, 66, 65.
20. Blanchot, *The Space of Literature,* 21, 23.
21. Blanchot, *The Space of Literature,* 22.
22. Blanchot, *The Space of Literature,* 41.
23. Blanchot, *The Space of Literature,* 66.
24. Blanchot, *The Space of Literature,* 32.
25. Blanchot, *Friendship,* 281.
26. Blanchot, *Friendship,* 291.
27. Maurice Blanchot, *The Book to Come,* trans. Charlotte Mandell (Stanford: Stanford University Press, 2003), 67.
28. Blanchot, *The Book to Come,* 67.
29. Blanchot, *The Book to Come,* 69.
30. Blanchot, *The Book to Come,* 76.
31. Blanchot, *The Book to Come,* 124.
32. Blanchot, *Friendship,* 238–39.
33. Blanchot, *Friendship,* 138.
34. David Whitehouse, "Origins of the Police," Libcom.org, December 24, 2014, https://libcom.org/history/origins-police-david-whitehouse.
35. Blanchot, *Friendship,* 139.
36. Lee Edelman, *No Future: Queer Theory and the Death Drive* (Durham: Duke University Press, 2004), 2.
37. Edelman, *No Future,* 2.
38. Edelman, *No Future,* 3.
39. Edelman, *No Future,* 3.
40. Edelman, *No Future,* 6.
41. Edelman, *No Future,* 21.
42. Edelman, *No Future,* 33, 35, 38.
43. Edelman, *No Future,* 101.

44. Edelman, *No Future,* 132.
45. Edelman, *No Future,* 114.
46. Edelman, *No Future,* 116.
47. Edelman, *No Future,* 154.
48. J. Halberstam, *The Queer Art of Failure* (Durham: Duke University Press, 2011), 106.
49. Halberstam, *The Queer Art of Failure,* 107.
50. Halberstam, *The Queer Art of Failure,* 108.
51. Sara Ahmed, *Queer Phenomenology: Orientations, Objects, Others* (Durham and London: Duke University Press, 2006), 173.
52. Bruce Bawer, *A Place at the Table: The Gay Individual in American Society* (New York: Simon & Schuster, 1994), quoted in Sara Ahmed, *Queer Phenomenology: Orientations, Objects, Others* (Durham: Duke University Press, 2006), 173.
53. Ahmed, *Queer Phenomenology*, 173.
54. Halberstam, *The Queer Art of Failure,* 27.
55. Halberstam, *The Queer Art of Failure*, 34, 73.
56. Halberstam, *The Queer Art of Failure*, 27.
57. Carolyn Dinshaw et al., "Theorizing Queer Temporalities: A Roundtable Discussion," *GLQ: A Journal of Lesbian and Gay Studies* 13, no. 2–3 (2007): 177–95, doi:10.1215/10642684-2006-030.
58. Dinshaw et al., "Theorizing Queer Temporalities," 181.
59. Halberstam, *The Queer Art of Failure,* 34.
60. Michael Warner, *The Trouble with Normal: Sex, Politics, and the Ethics of Queer Life* (Cambridge: Harvard University Press, 1999), 66.
61. Warner, *The Trouble with Normal*, 35.
62. Warner, *The Trouble with Normal,* 36.
63. José Esteban Muñoz, *Disidentifications: Queers of Color and the Performance of Politics* (Minneapolis: University of Minnesota Press, 1999), 106.

Chapter Four

Maturity as a Political Project

We all mature within a context, and where that context contains hierarchies, inequalities, and oppressions, these will affect us, both the oppressed and the privileged. The primary political divisions within society that I explore here are economic class, gender, and race. This certainly does not preclude other divisions and structures—these are merely three of the most operative divisions within contemporary American culture, the perspective from which I begin.

In *Justice and the Politics of Difference,*[1] Iris Marion Young defines injustice through oppression and defines structural oppression as the "disabling effects" on social groups. She begins her famous chapter on "the five faces of oppression"[2] by painting a picture of various social groups calling for justice: women's rights, Black rights, and Native rights, among others. It is here, in the midst of protest movements, that Young centers justice. Social groups call our attention to the injustices that they suffer, demanding that they be heard. For Young, justice is a plea from some social groups to others, necessary because we come from different contexts. Although this seems obvious, the background discipline from which I come (philosophy) has historically assumed that we can talk about some generic "universal human" when thinking about questions such as ethics, belief in god/s, the meaning of life, etc. For instance, when philosophers hash out ethical dilemmas such as the Trolley Problem—is it ethical to save one person at the expense of multiple lives? In which circumstances?—there is never any question as to the class of those pinned to the tracks, no question as to the gender or race of the train driver in relation to those about to die. But class, gender, and race have enormous impacts on how, when, and in which directions our maturing takes us. The context in which our social group/s are oppressed or privileged affects how we imagine our adult selves. And when we try to understand the maturity of others, we may wonder why their paths look different from ours. To understand the flaws of oneself, to imagine other ways of maturing, and to have a broader vision of society requires that we listen to the experiences of others and how oppression and privilege have structured their lives. Thus, a crucial part of justice is learning to become good listeners; a society of good listeners will be a society fighting oppression. As Young points out, protest happens precisely because listening to the oppressed groups has not happened until that point, making protest necessary. The demand is for open, critical listening and change.

Listening is a necessary (but not sufficient) part of justice. Since no one person experiences all possible types of injustice, we must listen to the experiences of others in order to understand how oppression disables the lives they desire to live. Young places herself within the field of critical theory precisely because of a dual acknowledgment: 1) our ideas begin from the concrete, material realities in which we find ourselves, and these realities must be investigated in order to find patterns of power and oppression in history and capital; and 2) our world can change. Nothing about the way the world is demands that it *must* be this way; critique implies the possibility of social change. I fully agree with Young on these points, and they structure the lens through which all subsequent comments in this chapter should be understood.

As Young argues that listening is crucial for justice, I argue that it is also crucial to maturity. For the same reason, listening might broaden our view of maturity beyond the experiences of the self. Perhaps it is helpful to return to Freud's notion of the id-ego-superego (see chapter 2). We might theorize that a person without a well-developed ego (in the sense of being resilient enough to move beyond) cannot be a good listener, and we might also theorize that such poor listeners do not come from all social groups equally. Herein lie the core questions of this chapter. The material realities embedded in society's structure will mean that some social groups contain better listeners with more resilient egos and superegos than other social groups, but which social groups and why? And what might we do to change this?

Social groups that have a history of oppression will have a different relationship to ego than those who have been privileged. Being privileged means being insulated from many problems and stresses. With enough money, one need not worry about arguing with the electric company to keep the lights on. If one is a White person in the United States, one need not worry much about being stopped by the police and that event turning into a nightmare. We might consider lists of privileges such as in Peggy McIntosh's "White Privilege: Unpacking the Invisible Knapsack,"[3] in which McIntosh lists the daily effects of living in a racist society with which Black individuals must wrestle and of which White people are generally ignorant. I have used such lists of privileges in teaching undergraduate students, and I find them to be generally helpful to White students, some of whom are woefully unaware of the experiences of Black people. On the other hand, these lists do deserve some of the criticism they receive. Some decolonial writers have pointed out that McIntosh's perspective stems from liberalism and focuses on the individual rather than grasping the history of systemic racism. Furthermore, the list focuses on White people and their perspective rather than on Black people. "Racism is now articulated not as oppression of people of colour, but as unearned advantages of white people. Moreover, racism is regarded as invisible by whites," and Whites need to be "taught" that racism exists and where to look for it from the individual perspective of their day-to-day lives.[4] But other writers have argued, and I largely agree, that "It's unfair to suggest that McIntosh thinks that individual self-awareness is the whole point of the privilege checklist exercise: it was always meant to point back to structural conditions."[5] Holding on to the critique of liberalism while seeing these lists of privileges can help people become better listeners to the world around them. But how do we inspire privileged people to listen and to care? How do we inspire them to mature in the sense of being open to other people and the world, especially when their survival (and even success) may not require them to do so? After all, we are asking them to do something they find uncomfortable and unnecessary.

The point is that there are people whose experiences are narrow in various ways. I myself was brought up in rural Iowa, where nearly everyone was White, lower-middle class or poor, Christian, and performing cisgender, heterosexual lives. I was, for example, woefully ignorant of the experiences of Black people, Jewish people, trans people, and wealthy people. In fact, I am just now learning about the power and connections that rich people have, how they often see themselves as above the law and beyond accountability, and this standpoint is new and shocking to me. Huge segments of the population, in the U.S. and elsewhere, may not come into contact with people unlike themselves. Furthermore, they may not have access to diverse culture and arts, as I did not. Such ignorance stymies our knowledge and our maturity. The maturity of each person (oppressed, privileged, and otherwise) depends upon our learning about different ways of thinking, seeing, and living. More important than merely being exposed to difference, we need to encounter people and experiences that profoundly challenge our ways of thinking.

LET US NOT ROMANTICIZE OPPRESSION

I am reminded of a story that Penn State philosophy professor Mariana Ortega recounted in 2017.[6] Ortega, whose experience of living through war largely shaped her thinking on oppression, once had a woman say to her, "I wish *I* had been in a war." As Ortega said, sometimes oppression undoes you, and it is not something to be sought as an experience of wisdom-gaining and maturity. Sometimes oppression does not help a person grow. It can make you retreat. It can bring you to self-hatred. It can make you brutal.

The romanticizing of oppression and oppressed groups is problematic. I should not say that the oppressed know something that I do not and valorize them on these grounds. As a professor at a Jesuit university, I find this problematic issue to be at the heart of the "mission service trips" with our faculty and students, usually run through our Campus Ministry offices. When I was a newer professor, I would often accompany students on these trips. The idea was to put students in contact with the "marginalized and oppressed of the world."[7] What this often felt like on the ground was what many people rightly call poverty tourism: We bring our American, middle class, mostly White students to visit sites of poverty and abjection, and the American students acquire an "experience" with poverty and walk away with a bit of First World Guilt. The breaking point for me was on a trip to rural India with 10 of our students. At the end of each day, we were expected to lead a reflection circle and discuss what we had seen and experienced that day. Going around the circle, one American student after another talked about how "grateful" and "blessed" they were to have a bed, access to sports equipment, plentiful food, and so on. I became angry. There was no talk about changing the structures of the systems that were keeping people in poverty. No talk of even questioning these systems. In the midst of my anger, it seemed to me that these students were gawking at the poor to make themselves feel better about their own lives. I doubt this was the full story, and I hold out hope that these kinds of trips do change students, at least later in life when they are able to carefully think through the experiences. Nonetheless, as I sat in a circle with American students in rural India, I viscerally felt the romanticizing of oppression, and I swore off such trips henceforth. The lesson should be that our encounter with otherness challenges us and thus changes the world as we become different kinds of people. It is possible that the "master" never stops being the master just because they have come to understand—or at least become "aware" of—the oppression of others, but rather than romanticizing the poor, such an encounter should make us want to rid the world of classist hierarchal structures.

According to Hegel, it is being challenged that inspires us to grow and prompts society to progress.[8] Challenge pushes us toward otherness and, thus, understanding at a higher level. If we follow a certain reading of Hegel, it will lead us to an odd position to seemingly claim that, on the whole, oppressed social groups are faced with more challenge and otherness and, therefore, are inspired to greater maturity than privileged groups. Would not we be pro-oppression, then, if we were looking to encourage maturity? This is similar to some readers of Hegel who claim that in the master-slave dialectic, the slave "wins" because the master knows only himself (and not very well at that), while the slave, due to conflict, must know himself, his master, and the dialectic between them; therefore, a slave has more wisdom and more maturity than the master. Yet, of course, this does not lead us to being pro-slavery. Is Hegel's thought even useful to us here?

Frantz Fanon's reading of Hegel might be helpful. He asks, what if my challenge is just a minor step in the eyes of the privileged? In *Black Skin, White Masks,* Fanon critiques Sartre's use of Hegel: "The theoretical and practical assertion of the supremacy of the white man is its thesis; the position of negritude as an antithetical value is the moment of negativity . . . it is intended to prepare the synthesis or realization of the human in a society without races."[9] Fanon resents being a step in the dialectic of White culture: "And, when I tried, on the level of ideas and intellectual activity, to reclaim my negritude . . . my effort was only a term in the dialectic."[10] Sartre's mistake is that he reduces Blackness to a stage that should be got beyond, thus robbing Blackness and Black culture of its import. The antithesis has to be full and real to be recognized. Fanon states that in the midst of his oppression and anger, "in the paroxysm of my being and my fury, he was reminding me that my blackness was only a minor term."[11] Fanon emphasizes that Black liberation is not a step in the dialectic of White culture.

But perhaps Hegel's work already takes this into consideration. Hegel writes that when there is a contradiction between two views and a dialectic is involved such that the two must meet and understand how each participates in Truth, it is not the case that the second step, that antithesis, is tossed away and moved past:

> But it is not truth as if the disparity had been thrown away, like dross from pure metal, not even like the tool which remains separate from the finished vessel; disparity, rather, as the negative, the self, is itself still directly present in the True as such. Yet we cannot therefore say that the false is a moment of the True, let alone a component part of it.[12]

For our purposes, this suggests that the experience of oppression merits attention as Truth in and of itself and not merely as a step on the way toward a higher goal, be that goal wisdom, understanding, or maturity.

Etienne Balibar also talks about the dialectical second step with regards to oppressed people and the need that this be recognized. In discussing the work of both Mary Wollstonecraft and Frantz Fanon, Balibar outlines the "synecdoche of the universal" as that which is both universal ("man" as in all of humanity) and particular ("man" as only males). "On the one hand," Balibar writes in *Citizen Subject: Foundations of Philosophical Anthropology*, "man is the whole of man; on the other, man is half of man."[13] In this case, women become

> identified with the organ (or faculty, distinctive quality) that she bears, or ultimately, with sexual difference itself. Man, on the contrary, tends to neutralize sexual difference; for men (males) can only appropriate the universal at the price of losing the sex attributed to woman. Nothing "remains" of man but reason and power—which are supposed to be asexual. In order to regain sex, he must *take possession of the woman* who bears it, which is why he educated her to offer it to him.[14]

We see here that women are only ever a step in the male universal dialectic because the masculine gender is supposed to be "generic," "unmarked," and "representative of the 'human' as such."[15] By Balibar's reading, Wollstonecraft is already aware of the synecdoche of this idea of "man" and plays with it in her work, and "Wollstonecraft's language anticipates all of these discourses."[16] This is similar to the dialectical structure seen in colonization: The White man owns universality and neutrality, so the Black man must join the White man's vision, the White man's world, the White man's dialectic. But, Balibar points out, "This has nothing to do with a contradiction between 'universalism' and 'particularism'; it is a matter of the contradiction that affects the very utterance of the universal" since neither Wollstonecraft nor Fanon "speak *about* difference in order to define it, justify it, or combat it; they speak *in* difference (or *out* of difference) of the contradiction that it induces."[17]

Why, then, care about the issue of oppressed groups being relegated to the antithetical moment within the project of maturity? Because it is relevant to the majority of people, oppressed and privileged, but also for society as a whole to mature and to become the context where critical, conscious maturity is encouraged. Oppressed people cannot mature if they are not recognized. Likewise, privileged people will be ignorant and childish with respect to their own world. Hegel writes that "Self-consciousness exists in and for itself when, and by the fact that, it so exists for another; that is, it exists only in being acknowledged" and "It receives back its own self."[18] We do not have an account of who we are; in fact, we do not even have a *who* (an "I") without others. The more otherness I engage with, the more of a self I become. Other people help us create and understand the self as a separate entity in the world.

ON RECOGNITION AND REFUSAL

What happens when I give others recognition but they refuse to recognize me? This is the situation in Hegel's "lord and bondsman" (master and slave) dialectic. The lord (master) does not recognize the bondsman (slave) but the bondsman must recognize the lord, which is asymmetrical recognition. If we apply this to social groups, we see these asymmetrical relations between social groups with privilege and those without, those with more power and those with less. Injustice in the world prevents those with privilege from maturing. Fanon quotes an American friend who said to him, "The presence of the Negroes beside the whites is in a way an insurance policy on humanness. When the whites feel that they have become too mechanized, they turn to the men of color and ask them for a little human sustenance."[19] Fanon deems this the lowest level of recognition, but at least some kind of recognition: "I was no longer a zero" but "my originality had been torn out of me" and "haunted by a galaxy of erosive stereotypes" such as "the Negro's sui generis good nature."[20] Then Fanon quotes his teacher Aimé Césaire, who called the disenfranchised "Gentle men, polite, considerate, unquestionably superior to those who tortured them."[21] Césaire seems to put the oppressed at a higher place, but it is not the duty of oppressed people to help the privileged develop. The queer person is under no obligation to help normative people develop, women under no obligation to help men, Black people under no obligation to help Whites. We must be careful, then, not to imply that maturing is solely the responsibility of the individuals themselves. We must insist that as a society, we are all under the duty to help everyone develop and mature. The question becomes how to get the privileged to see what they cannot see without making this the duty of the oppressed.

Fanon's work concerns the effects of colonization, and again, the oppressed side of the power division is referred to and treated as children. The colonizer is the adult, the one who brings knowledge, civilization, law and order, and the colonized are "beasts" and "children" who need to be taken care of. Fanon writes in *The Wretched of the Earth* that Western values are seen as the mature and progressive ones, whereas the native does not even know how to take care of himself or his neighborhood—"the stink of the native quarter, of breeding swarms, of foulness," "distended bodies which are like nothing on earth," "children who belong to nobody."[22] Moreover, the colonizers are treated as individuals while the colonized are treated as a "mass."[23] Fanon uses the colonizer's language of "underdeveloped countries," which implies that there is some directionality or teleology that a country must follow in order to reach the individuation of men.[24]

In Silvia Federici's research on witch trials at the dawn of capitalism, her primary interest is particularly in poor, old, unmarried, and sexually active women because these were the vast majority tortured and killed as witches. This logic of murderous intimidation as a tool for "putting people in their place" was also used around the same time (1550–1650) as a means to discipline colonized peoples. Federici writes how "New World witch hunting was a deliberate strategy used by the authorities to instill terror, destroy collective resistance, silence entire communities, and turn their members against each other."[25] As with women, the strategy was to denigrate others "to the point where identification is precluded."[26] Federici gives accounts of Native Americans and enslaved Africans labeled and murdered as "demons" and "devils" by colonizers throughout North, Central, and South America to show that "the destinies of women in Europe and those of Amerindians and Africans in the colonies" were "connected" and the influences were "reciprocal."[27] The ideologies of witchcraft and racism were explicitly tied together by powerful White men who sought authority and capital, with the demand to expand their power without interference. The strategy works because once you systematically torture and kill some people in each community, everyone begins living under a regime of terror and fear, forcing most to play by the rules of the colonizers, often even turning against their own communities. In the case of the Andes, the colonizing Spaniards outlawed their religious practices, gods (*huacas*), and many traditional ways of life. For instance, they outlawed polygamy: "Ironically, while polygamous unions were dissolved, with the arrival of the Spaniards, no aboriginal woman was safe from rape," and, in fact, soon after polygamy was outlawed, prostitution thrived, making women's sexuality focused not on themselves and their own desires but on the needs and desires of men.[28] Of course, once a woman was perceived as (or was) a sex worker, the colonizing Europeans made the same charges against them that they were making against women in their home countries at the time, that these sex workers were witches attempting to destroy the potency of men. Life became so difficult that "at times it was the 'Indian' men themselves who delivered their female kin to the priests or *encomenderos* in exchange for some economic reward or public post."[29] Turning community members against each other is a much-used way to break any solidarity that might threaten the power of the colonizers.

A gripping account of how this logic played out in colonial Africa was created by Mauritian director Med Hondo in the 1970 film *Soleil Ô (Oh, Sun)*.[30] In the first 10 minutes of the film, Hondo dramatizes French colonization. A White man is seen with a group of about 10 Black men; first, the White man brings in his religion (Catholicism) and baptizes them all, then he brings in his violent order (the military) and all the Black men are enlisted as soldiers. The same prop that was used as a wooden cross is turned on its side and becomes a gun for the Black soldiers. There is an easy transition from worshipping the White man's god to killing. Once the White man gives the Black men the weapons, he convinces them to distrust each other, pays them money to kill each other, and in the end, nearly all of the Black men are dead, while the White man stands above their prone bodies, taking back the bills of money he had paid them and stashing them in his own pocket as he smiles and lights a cigar. Fear—in this case the fear of White people by colonized peoples—is an excellent way to turn a community against itself, to cause them to distrust one another, and dissuade or prevent people from expanding their knowledge and abilities to analyze their historical and material situation. Fear often blocks thinking.

Hegel talks about the life or death struggle, which occurs when a subject himself wants to be the center of universality. He writes in *Phenomenology of Spirit,* "The two do not reciprocally give and receive one another back from each other consciously, but leave each other free only indifferently, like things."[31] Hegel calls this an "abstract negation," not a real negation, because a real negation takes the other seriously. In fact, it accepts what the other is with some depth. It is here that Hegel begins to talk about "the lord and bondsman."[32] "Each is indeed certain of its own self, but not of the other, and therefore its own self-certainty still has no truth."[33] Think of this in relation to modern-day incels, "involuntarily celibate" men who believe that women are of a different species and that men are entitled to women's bodies. These men do not recognize women and, therefore, they do not recognize themselves; the object they want so badly does not recognize them and so they shun "it."

Judith Butler offers an addition to Hegel on this point. One might say that once we have experienced oppression, we are in a better place to understand human vulnerability. Grasping our condition as one based in our common vulnerability can be the basis for care and compassion. However, not all people or social groups experience vulnerability to the same degree. We all start life as vulnerable infants and small children, but negotiating vulnerability throughout life is the task of some more than others. In *Precarious Life: The Powers of Mourning and Violence,* Butler confirms that "Women know this question well, have known it in nearly all times."[34] But, for many people, once they grow up, they begin to believe in fantasies of autonomy. And, as Butler emphasizes, "A vulnerability must be perceived and recognized in order to come into play in an ethical encounter, and there is no guarantee that this will happen."[35]

ON VULNERABILITY, MASCULINITY, AND GENDER ROLES

The documentary film *The Work*[36] depicts intensive group therapy at the maximum-security Folsom Prison. It is a film centered on masculinity and its devastating effects on men. The prisoners have been convicted of murder, robbery, rape, assault, and other violent crimes, and each prisoner is a man who struggles with emotions and relationships. This movie seems an illustration of the idea that violence is often an inability to grasp and articulate one's feelings. One prisoner, a former gang member convicted of murder, wants to be able to grieve the death of his sister and has not been able to. He longs to get behind his thick armor and reach his emotions (like "gold coins") that his conscious, everyday life as a man will not let him access. All of the men in group therapy struggle with not being able to express love and connection, and each feels betrayed by fathers, mothers, friends, and mentors. Their life experiences have taught them that it is not acceptable to be vulnerable and seek connection. They have not been able to get beyond those experiences, and their lives of violence seem (at least in part) a response to their lack of openness to express care and vulnerability. The group therapy works as a kind of communal act of growth and maturing, where they all help each other move in the direction of being more open. Men hardened by life experiences and gang membership share their fears and weaknesses, cry together, hold each other, and recount painful childhood memories.

Here we have an example of the effects of inequality from the privileged side of the hierarchy. Despite patriarchy's power over women and all of men's advantages, masculinity is clearly harming men as well. Patriarchy has debilitating effects on men who are expected to live inside the stifling role of masculinity.

While teaching existentialism in an "Introduction to Philosophy" course, I asked students to write short papers about bad faith and transcendence, linking these ideas to specific times in their lives when they have been pressured to fulfill a role. I asked students to interrogate when, why, and how they thought about the bad faith of that role. This particular class contained many 18- and 19-year-old male athletes, and I expected to find hypermasculine posturing in their papers. I was happily proven wrong! All but one of these men spoke of how they struggled with the masculine sports-star role, how they felt pressured and even taunted by fathers, uncles, and friends into that role, and how they were just now beginning to see that this view had warped their own happiness and liberation. Like the men in Folsom Prison, they talked achingly about missed connections and love. One student wrote that his father and brothers had always played American football, but he himself didn't like the sport and so fell into lacrosse instead; although lacrosse is one of the most "macho" sports at my college, this student explained that he had never felt macho enough for the other men in his family. This is how roles work, of course. No one ever fulfills them entirely. There is difficulty on both paths, in leaving the role or attempting to stay. Leaving it alongside supportive others (as the men did in group therapy in *The Work*, or as it has happened in queer communities) is the best of a no-win situation.

Regarding this double bind with regards to gender roles, Julia Kristeva writes in her article "Women's Time" that there are two ways for women to relate to the symbolic order: Women must choose between the sacrifice of taking up the feminine role or the violence of trying to leave it (although in her view, there is no way to leave it entirely, but one can attempt to "burst it").[37] Kristeva's view, however, does not leave room for the change we have actually witnessed. Gender roles are not and never have been static, and the more women we see as senators and the more men we see wearing make-up, the more we will chip away at these roles.

ON GENDER AND RACE

In *Women, Race and Class*, Angela Davis outlines how various structural oppressions relate. While the book is mostly a historical account of these structures (especially within the context of the early United States), it bears attention in understanding how we got to where we are today (and where we might go in the future), which is to be attuned to how a culture changes in a Hegelian/Marxist sense. I want to discuss how sex and gender structure our experience of maturing, but we also need to be attuned to the fact that not all people within a social group (in this case "women") deal with the exact same issues. Davis indicates the ways in which slavery shaped differences between Black and White women in the United States. Both were under the mastery of White men, but their positions were markedly different.[38] Black women were treated (and traded) similarly to Black men, valued for their ability to work. Wealthy White women, on the other hand, were treated like dolls or trophies. Whereas Black women were valued for their strength, White women were valued for their fragility. Black women were to be worked, White women were to be treated like children. Davis's narrative is instructive because it shows how the category of "women" is not a category of sameness. One cannot understand the category of sex without also understanding the categories of race and class.

So, if we wonder why the feminine ideal of White women is obsession with youth, cuteness, and even stupidity, Davis can help us understand. It has been well established in dominant culture that intelligence and strength in men is rewarded while in women it is often punished. Studies have shown that the more and higher degrees that women achieve, the less attractive they become to straight men, whereas the reverse is true for men.[39] As Jack Halberstam writes, "Stupidity in women, as we know, is often expected in this male-dominated culture, and some women cultivate it because they see it rewarded . . ."[40] In *The Second Sex,* Simone de Beauvoir writes that to be attractive has never meant the same thing for men and women. In White, heterosexual life, women are valued for seeming naive, silly, and weak, and even women's clothing is supposed to demonstrate that women are fragile. For a man, on the other hand, being powerful, smart, and accomplished is the goal, and "for him neither elegance nor beauty constitutes him as object; thus he does not usually consider his appearance a reflection of his being."[41] Whether straight White women wear this mask as a persona or whether they believe in it makes little difference to an existentialist—the action creates the norm.

MELANCHOLY AND IDENTIFICATION WITH THE ENEMY

A serious threat to the class consciousness and growth of oppressed groups is our tendency to identify with those who have power. Sara Ahmed makes the point in *Queer Phenomenology: Orientations, Objects, Others* that the melancholic identifies with what repudiates them.[42] For instance, with regards to race, Ahmed (herself of mixed racial background) writes that "the desire to be white for a mixed race child is melancholic" and that "whiteness was certainly 'at home' even if I did not possess it."[43] Ideology convinces us that we should identify with the views, ideas, heroics, traumas, and existential angst of heterosexual White men. Although the majority of us are not that man, we have been formed to experience the world the way they do. Joan Smith's book *Misogynies,* and specifically her essay on Milan Kundera, made me consider this idea more fully.

When I was in my early 20s, I was a big fan of Kundera's work. Reviewers praise his "intellectually acceptable" sexuality and his "love of eroticism, fantasy and fun."[44] Smith, however, indicates that it is Kundera's violent misogyny that passes as intellectual sexuality. It is the "passing" part of this that troubles me, because it passed for me, too. I began to see his work differently after reading Smith. She goes through several images in Kundera's writing that detail how disgusting he finds women, how his sexuality involves demeaning them. This is most pronounced when the protagonist is female and when Kundera assumes that women's sexuality has to do with enjoying their own debasement, being belittled and denigrated. "The issue, as one might expect, is power; each time a character in a Kundera novel pours scorn on the female body, he or she . . . is denying the fear that the body inspires" and "proving his mastery," elucidates Smith.[45]

What Smith writes of Kundera also applies to many other male authors whose work I used to read and love (in particular, Philip Roth and Ernest Hemingway). I was a philosophy student and a feminist, yet early in my life I read their novels voraciously and with much appreciation. Why? How were my mind and my positionality in the world framed in order for me to identify with straight White men? To think that the debasement and disrespect of my own gender was the very definition of erotic? If most of us repeatedly identify with straight White men through their overrepresentation in media, literature, politics, and business, it makes sense that our own disorientation may take us by surprise. We can be thrown off by a realization that our own embodiment does not align with the way we have been framed to see and experience the world and ourselves in it. This surprise is what Maurice Merleau-Ponty calls a break between seeing and being seen, the hand-shake of touching and being touched assumed to be reciprocal.[46]

There is none of this kind of reciprocity for those who are not in the dominant group, for those who suffer from a lack of representation (or weak and one-dimensional representation) as protagonists of the most loved cultural texts. For many hours of the day, in my inner life, I may experience the world the way the hero of a Kundera novel does. And then some guy talks over me at a meeting and I am reminded, "Oh yeah: I am a woman. I forgot. I will be given little respect." And it stings every time. Culture, and especially my field of philosophy, has trained me to assume the existence of some generic human being without gender, sexuality, class, ability, race, etc., who, in reality, always turns out to be a straight, able-bodied, White man. This universal human being making choices between utilitarianism and virtue ethics has never been a generic human, but when you read enough novels, watch enough movies, and study enough philosophy, you start seeing yourself as that so-called generic human. Somehow it is always a surprise that the world never treats you as such.

ON CAPITALIST REALISM AND CRITICAL REFLECTION

One of the deepest ways in which our maturity and health—especially our mental health—are politically affected is by class, specifically class under capitalism. In *Playing and Reality*, Donald Winnicott looks at society according to its healthiness. He admits that there could be times when the number of unhealthy persons is high and, in that case, "the social unit becomes itself a psychiatric casualty."[47] We must reproach Winnicott here, for he might not think that society was so "psychiatrically healthy" if he were a woman, a member of the lower class, a person of color, or a queer person. And this brings us to the work of Mark Fisher, who does not believe that capitalist society is psychiatrically healthy. Fisher's *Capitalist Realism* pays particular attention to the intersections of mental health and capitalism: "Mental health, in fact, is a paradigm case of how capitalist realism operates. Capitalist realism insists on treating mental health as if it were a natural fact, like weather (but, then again, weather is no longer a natural fact so much as a political-economic effect)."[48] Fisher argues that "madness is not a natural but a political category."[49] He notes that depression is the most treated condition in the British health care system and in the U.S., with approximately 50 percent of the population at one time or another taking anti-depressants. Knowing this, it is absurd to think that the causes of depression are individual, "as if they were caused only by chemical imbalances in the individual's neurology and/or by their family background."[50] Rather, we should be considering the "question of social systemic causation" and understand that it is "necessary to reframe the growing problem of stress (and distress) in capitalist societies."[51]

But why have we accepted this situation? Why do we carry on prescribing more and more meds? Why do we as a society accept the "privatization of stress," and, Fisher wants us to ask, "how has it become acceptable that so many people, and especially so many young people, are ill?"[52] If we take depression, attention deficit hyperactivity disorder, and dyslexia all together, we face a plague of capitalist affects—"If, then, something like attention deficit hyperactivity disorder is a pathology, it is a pathology of late capitalism."[53] Fisher claims that "It is not an exaggeration to say that being a teenager in late capitalist Britain is now close to being reclassified as a sickness."[54]

There is another, newer mental health crisis on the rise that affects mostly younger people: climate anxiety. Climate catastrophe and global warming are inextricably linked to capitalism. How could a political-economic system that requires endless profit *not* destroy soil, air, water, food, weather patterns, and, ultimately, all life? It was inevitable that capitalism would lead to environmental ruin. Marx thought that class consciousness and revolution would save us, but later Marxists (like Herbert Marcuse) understood that our species caused environmental crisis before we caused a political revolution. We now know that we have passed the point where we might avert climate crisis. It is here. It gets worse every day, especially in the form of increasing storms and fires. Even if we began major structural and individual changes and upended capitalism soon, it would still be too late to avoid climate catastrophes. This should not cause inaction, as we could still mitigate the situation to some degree and attenuate the rate of collapse of life on the planet. Yet, reality is grim, especially looking forward. Psychologists have begun to talk about anxiety and trauma caused by climate catastrophe:

> For Elizabeth Wathuti, a climate activist from Kenya, her experience of climate anxiety is not so much about the future but what is happening now. "People in African countries experience eco-anxiety differently because climate change for us is about the impacts that we are already experiencing now and the possibilities of the situation getting worse," she said. . . . A common worry she hears among students is: "We won't die of old age, we'll die from climate change."[55]

Greta Thunberg has wisely told us that adults, especially leaders, "are behaving like children" with regards to ecological crisis.[56] The older generations caused these eco-crises, we continue to exacerbate them, and we do not properly acknowledge or critically reflect upon it. Generally, we ignore the issue or deflect it onto others. Neither are mature responses to crisis. We need large structural changes to support public transportation, solar and wind energy, and sustainable farming, and we need to end all government subsidies for coal, oil, and animal agriculture. Unfortunately, we are moving in the opposite direction. In January 2022, President Joe Biden introduced a plan to give $1 billion in subsidies to animal agriculture and meat processing plants, one of the largest (if not the largest) contributors to global warming.[57] It is no wonder that people are beginning to suffer from climate anxiety as we witness the continuance of practices that are causing our own ruin.

Health problems caused by late capitalism include anxiety, depression, ADHD, climate anxiety, suicide, heart disease, cancer, diabetes, etc. When these issues are taken together, they affect more than half the population, particularly those ages 12–30. But what about the winners in this political landscape, those without mental or physical hardships? What about those who grow up perceived as adults with all the normative signs of success? Let us talk about the maturity of people deemed to be leaders in late capitalism. For example, most university leaders with whom I am in contact have a curious lack of integrity, which seems so pervasive that it must be more than an individual ethical or mental health problem. Describing the management culture of late capitalism, Fisher gives an example from his own experience:

> He asserted with full confidence a story about the college and its future one day—what the implications of the inspection were likely to be; what senior management was thinking; then *literally the next day* would happily propound a story that directly contradicted what he previously said. There was never a question of his *repudiating* the previous story; it was as if he only dimly remembered there ever being another story. This, I suppose, is "good management."[58]

Possibly, because we hope to have a conflict-free and "pleasant" work place, we, a community of workers, begin to accept these variations of the story, these cracks in an integrated reality. Most people learn simply to ignore what our leaders say, or to accept it cheerfully, from one day to the next, only dimly aware of contradictions. Cynicism and acceptance of this as normal begin to settle in, as otherwise one would be constantly angry. Still, Fisher asks, "How could it ever be possible for us to believe successive or even co-extensive stories that so obviously contradict one another?"[59] Managers must cultivate the ability to see reality as fungible under capitalist imperatives—they must be flexible in order to seem (and think of themselves as) kind and wise while at the same time being unkind and unwise. In other words, "forgetting becomes an adaptive strategy."[60] Such obvious contradictions in managers rarely seem to call their sanity into question. "On the face of it," Fisher writes, "this manager is a model of beaming mental health, his whole being radiating a hail-fellow-well-met bonhomie. Such cheerfulness can only be maintained if one has a near-total absence of any critical reflexivity."[61]

Recall the question introduced earlier: What is the difference between normative estimations of maturity and what we might call critical and political maturity? Taking Fisher's ideas into account, they seem to be almost opposite. People who rise through the ranks of a capitalist hierarchy, who become executives, leaders, and so forth, are often lacking the most important aspect of maturity, the aspect that opens up all other important characteristics: critical reflection. To be "realistic" in this world is to shut off the possibility of critical reflection.

This brings up a terrible practicality for parents, teachers, friends, therapists, and all of us who are co-responsible for the maturing of ourselves and others. Should we advise young people that they will be more mature if, in fact, they *do not* succeed in this sick society? In a way, yes. But, most importantly, we must be part of activist movements that will change the society. We need to make our political reality a context where mature and critically reflective persons can be connected, interdependent, and both supported and challenged by others. If we are not activists working toward that world, then we are also immature, having given in to a cynical acceptance of *what is*, a sure sign that we, too, lack critical reflection.

NOTES

1. Iris Marion Young, *Justice and the Politics of Difference* (Princeton: Princeton University Press, 1990).
2. Young, *Justice and the Politics of Difference*, 39–64.
3. Peggy McIntosh, "White Privilege: Unpacking the Invisible Knapsack," *Peace and Freedom Magazine* (July/August 1989): 10–12, https://psychology.umbc.edu/files/2016/10/White-Privilege_McIntosh-1989.pdf.
4. Sandew Hira, "A Decolonial Critique of the Concept of White Privilege: Why Injustice is Not a Privilege," *Decolonial International Network,* 2017, https://din.today/a-decolonial-critique-of-the-concept-of-white-privilege-why-injustice-is-not-a-privilege/.
5. Jacqui Shine, "Sympathy for the White Devil: Phoebe Maltz Bovy's 'The Perils of Privilege,'" *Los Angeles Review of Books*, April 16, 2017, https://lareviewofbooks.org/article/sympathy-for-the-white-devil-phoebe-maltz-bovys-the-perils-of-privilege/.
6. Mariana Ortega, at the 18th Annual Meeting of the Phenomenology Roundtable, San Antonio, TX, May 31–June 2, 2017, https://phenomenologyroundtable.wordpress.com/2017/11/05/18th-annual-phenomenology-roundtable-meeting/.
7. Pedro Arrupe, "Men for Others: Training Agents of Change for the Promotion of Justice; Father Arrupe's Address to the International Congress of Jesuit Alumni of Europe, Valencia, Spain, July 31, 1973," in *Justice with Faith Today: Selected Letters and Addresses—II*, ed. Jerome Aixala (St. Louis: The Institute of Jesuit Sources,

1980), 123–38, https://jesuitportal.bc.edu/research/documents/1973_arrupemenforothers/.

8. Georg Wilhelm Friedrich Hegel, *Phenomenology of Spirit,* trans. A. V. Miller (Oxford: Oxford University Press, 1977).

9. Frantz Fanon, *Black Skin, White Masks* (New York: Grove Press, 1967), 133.

10. Fanon, *Black Skin, White Masks,* 132.

11. Fanon, *Black Skin, White Masks,* 138.

12. Hegel, *Phenomenology of Spirit*, 23.

13. Etienne Balibar, *Citizen Subject: Foundations of Philosophical Anthropology* (New York: Fordham University Press, 2017), 283.

14. Balibar, *Citizen Subject,* 283.

15. Balibar, *Citizen Subject,* 284.

16. Balibar, *Citizen Subject,* 284.

17. Balibar, *Citizen Subject,* 286.

18. Hegel, *Phenomenology of Spirit,* 111.

19. Fanon, *Black Skin, White Masks,* 129.

20. Fanon, *Black Skin, White Masks,* 129.

21. Fanon, *Black Skin, White Masks,* 130.

22. Frantz Fanon, *The Wretched of the Earth* (New York: Grove Press, 1963), 42–43.

23. Fanon, *The Wretched of the Earth,* 47.

24. Fanon, *The Wretched of the Earth,* 181.

25. Silvia Federici, *Caliban and the Witch: Women, the Body and Primitive Accumulation* (New York: Autonomedia, 2004), 220.

26. Federici, *Caliban and the Witch,* 221.

27. Federici, *Caliban and the Witch,* 198.

28. Federici, *Caliban and the Witch,* 230.

29. Federici, *Caliban and the Witch,* 230.

30. *Soleil Ô (Oh, Sun)*, directed by Med Hondo (France / Mauritania, 1970), screened at the 2020 Berlin International Film Festival, https://www.berlinale.de/en/archive-selection/archive-2020/programme/detail/202012225.html.

31. Hegel, *Phenomenology of Spirit,* 114.

32. Hegel, *Phenomenology of Spirit,* 115.

33. Hegel, *Phenomenology of Spirit,* 113.

34. Judith Butler, *Precarious Life: The Powers of Mourning and Violence* (London: Verso, 2004), 42.

35. Butler, *Precarious Life,* 43.

36. *The Work,* directed by Jairus McLeary and Gethin Aldous (Blanketfort Media, 2017).

37. Julia Kristeva, "Women's Time," trans. Alice Jardine and Harry Blake, in *The Kristeva Reader*, ed. Toril Moi (New York: Columbia, 1986), 187–213.

38. Angela Y. Davis, *Women, Race and Class* (New York: Vintage Books, 1983).

39. Robinson Meyer, "Dude, She's (Exactly 25 Percent) Out of Your League," *The Atlantic*, August 10, 2018, https://www.theatlantic.com/science/archive/2018/08/online-dating-out-of-your-league/567083/.

40. J. Halberstam, *The Queer Art of Failure* (Durham: Duke University Press, 2011), 57.

41. Simone de Beauvoir, *The Second Sex*, trans. Constance Borde and Sheila Malovany-Chevallier (New York: Vintage Books, 2011), 572.

42. Sara Ahmed, *Queer Phenomenology: Orientations, Objects, Others* (Durham and London: Duke University Press, 2006), 174.

43. Ahmed, *Queer Phenomenology,* 146–47.

44. Joan Smith, *Misogynies* (London: Westbourne Press, 1989), 114.

45. Smith, *Misogynies*, 117.

46. Maurice Merleau-Ponty, *Phenomenology of Perception*, trans. Donald A. Landes (New York: Routledge, 2012).

47. Donald Woods Winnicott, *Playing and Reality* (New York: Routledge Classics, 2005), 190.

48. Mark Fisher, *Capitalist Realism: Is There No Alternative?* (Winchester: Zero Books, John Hunt Publishing, 2009), 19.

49. Fisher, *Capitalist Realism,* 19.

50. Fisher, *Capitalist Realism,* 21.

51. Fisher, *Capitalist Realism,* 21, 19.

52. Fisher, *Capitalist Realism,* 19.

53. Fisher, *Capitalist Realism,* 25.

54. Fisher, *Capitalist Realism,* 21.

55. Matthew Taylor and Jessica Murray, "'Overwhelming and Terrifying': The Rise of Climate Anxiety," *The Guardian*, February 10, 2020, https://www.theguardian.com/environment/2020/feb/10/overwhelming-and-terrifying-impact-of-climate-crisis-on-mental-health.

56. Damian Carrington, "'Our Leaders Are Like Children,' School Strike Founder Tells Climate Summit," *The Guardian*, December 4, 2018, https://www.theguardian.com/environment/2018/dec/04/leaders-like-children-school-strike-founder-greta-thunberg-tells-un-climate-summit.

57. Jake Johnson, "House Progressives Hail Biden Moves to Combat Meat Industry 'Price Gouging,'" *Common Dreams*, January 4, 2022, https://www.commondreams.org/news/2022/01/04/house-progressives-hail-biden-moves-combat-meat-industry-price-gouging.

58. Fisher, *Capitalist Realism,* 54.

59. Fisher, *Capitalist Realism,* 55.

60. Fisher, *Capitalist Realism,* 56.

61. Fisher, *Capitalist Realism,* 56.

Chapter Five

The Family Is a Political Structure

"The term family *was first used by the Romans to denote a social unit the head of which ruled over wife, children, and slaves—under Roman law he was invested with rights of life and death over them all;* famulus *means domestic slave, and* familia *is the total number of slaves belonging to one man."*

— Shulamith Firestone[1]

The family is political. Many people think that the private family is a safe haven of unconditional love separated from political strife, but feminists long ago taught us that *the personal is political*. Marriage and family structure are political inventions and developments. Politics is not merely what national governments do or do not do; there is the politics of who washes the dishes in the household, who has or organizes the capital, who is dependent on whom for life's necessities, and, most importantly, who is free to leave and who is not. The family is, furthermore, one of the primary sites of our maturing. Families based on the politics of patriarchy will consciously or unconsciously raise children to be patriarchal. The patriarchal family is hegemonic. Our celebrations surrounding family lifestyle choices (engagements, baby showers, wedding anniversaries) support the hegemonic view, since reverse lifestyle choices are not celebrated but ignored or mourned as failures. If we want to live in a world that allows persons to develop into open, critical-thinking people committed to a just and caring society, we need a different understanding and praxis of family.

A close-to-home example to frame the theme of the family as an ideological institution: Many people of all genders have trouble envisioning women as leaders, intellectuals, or artists. (I offer this example nonetheless suspicious of the concept of "leadership" per se.) Within patriarchy, most people have understood women to be primary caretakers in the family and men to be authorities in the broader world. When women political candidates exist, many refuse to vote for them or judge their actions and policies more harshly than similar actions and policies of male candidates. As a woman professor, I struggle with a related issue because students unconsciously expect me to be kinder and more nurturing than their male professors—again, expectations first modeled by the gendered power dynamic of the nuclear, patriarchal family. Student evaluation research backs this up: Students expect male professors to be knowledgeable experts in their fields, whereas students expect female professors to be warm and friendly rather than experts in their fields. And when female professors are not warm and friendly, students evaluate them harshly on the basis of those failures in nurturing. Students also doubt the expertise of female professors. Routinely, 18-year-old male students who have never studied philosophy mansplain to me about what texts should or should not be read in a philosophy course. My male colleagues report little to none of that. Attitudes toward women start in the family and stem from experiences we have before we can speak or understand what they mean. Those memories/ideologies are hard to access and, thus, hard to destroy. In *The Dialectic of Sex: The Case for Feminist Revolution,* Shulamith Firestone follows Marx in noting that "the family contained within itself in embryo all the antagonisms that later develop on a wide scale within the society and the state."[2] Friedrich Engels notes that inequality begins in the family and that "the first division of labour" is "based on sex," which means that we cannot have a socialist revolution until we first tackle the problem of the family.[3] Or, as Firestone powerfully argues, "For unless revolution uproots the basic social organization—the biological family—the vinculum through which the psychology of power can always be smuggled—the tapeworm of exploitation will never be annihilated."[4] If we would destroy gender inequality, we must destroy the hegemonic family as it exists and build more egalitarian care structures.

Anecdotally, when I attended university in the 1990s, it seemed that fewer women opted to get married in a patriarchal way that included diamond rings, being proposed to, being "given away" by their father, or changing their last name. Yet, a study in 2017 found that 70 percent of Americans (women and men both) believe that women ought to change their last names when married, with 50 percent believing that it should be required by law.[5] On a not-unrelated note, the United States Supreme Court reversed abortion rights in 2022, and some have even suggested rolling back rights to contraception.[6] These shifts cannot be accidental. A return to conservative gender roles must have roots in a wider political context. Sophie Lewis suggests in *Full Surrogacy Now: Feminism Against Family* that it could be fears of impending global warming that unconsciously cause people to scurry backwards into traditional roles within the family: "we have no choice but to understand this compulsion toward reproductive self-deferral as the deep sublimate depression of a world in eco-catastrophe."[7] At the same time, paradoxically, normative family practices such as birthing many human beings (which is often a result of a lack of access to abortion and birth control) are actions perpetuating climate crisis and crowding out and extinguishing other species on the planet. We fall back into what we may believe to be the "comfort" of the known, but it is precisely that *known* that has brought us to the catastrophe we face.

Silvia Federici's discussion of the transition to capitalism brilliantly shows how political context shapes family ideology and our desires. This transitional process required that new forms of discipline and work be imposed on the populace, and witch-hunts (mostly between 1550–1650) became a method of achieving it. There "was the need of the European elites to eradicate an entire mode of existence which, by the late Middle Ages, was threatening their political and economic power."[8] Hence, "When this task was accomplished—when social discipline was restored, and the ruling class saw its hegemony consolidated—witch trials came to an end."[9] In reading Parinetto, Federici says that "the witch-hunt was a classical instance in the history of capitalism (unfortunately not the last) of how 'going back' was a means of stepping forward from the viewpoint of capital."[10] The contemporary movement wherein people choose patriarchal marriages and nuclear families could also be seen as a "going back" in order to shore up hegemonic power at a time when capitalism is unstable.

Lewis agrees that the present day is marked, in the Western world, by an attempt to sanctify and impose White, bourgeois, patriarchal family values. As we saw in our reading of Angela Davis, Lewis states that "Historically, motherhood in the United States was elaborated as an institution of married white womanhood. Thus, black enslaved women could make no claims of kinship or property to the fruits of their gestational labors . . . while other eugenic and patriarchal laws dispossessed unwed proletariats."[11] The family defined as a private, biological grouping of daddy, mommy, and babies is a norm that never existed for many, including Black Americans under slavery, Native Americans whose children were taken from their communities, queer or incarcerated people who were seen as improper parents, and poor women without access to birth control and abortion.

Capitalism is shaky in these times, and violence against women, compounded by racism and transphobia, has increased globally and within the U.S.[12] In *Witches, Witch-Hunting, and Women*, Federici gives examples of modern-day witch hunts and the mass killing of women, especially older women, in certain African countries, the disappearance and murders of First Nations women in Canada, and the increase in human trafficking globally.

Furthermore, "In the United States, where since the 1980s the murders of women have been steadily rising, with more than three thousand women killed each year, the murders of women of color are less likely to receive media attention or be solved than the murders of white women."[13] Federici's analysis demonstrates that whenever capitalists have needed to shore up power, there has been a move to discipline the culture, starting with the women. This was the case from 1550–1650 at the birth of capitalism, and it has continued to happen periodically whenever there is a threat to the social status quo or a movement of experimenting with other ways of living. Women pose a threat to the status quo because of "what women represent in their capacity to keep their communities together and, equally important, to defend noncommercial conceptions of security and wealth."[14] With capitalism on shaky ground, especially since 2008, and with the ruling class sensing a threat, we are simultaneously witnessing horrific violence against women and a sentimental cultural return to traditional marriage and family.

The fact that many women choose exploitation does not cancel the exploitation itself, as our "choosing" is never fully conscious and always takes place within a social and political context. When capital needs war planes (as the U.S. did during World War II), it constructs womanhood on the narrative of women being excellent engineers and factory workers, and if capital needs babies and the reification of masculine authority, it casts womanhood in the image of the housewife and the mother in a subservient family structure.[15]

Throughout the history of capitalism in the United States, the nuclear family and its gender roles were *invented* at a particular time but set up to appear universal and natural. Indeed, households have always existed, as a "household" is simply an "income pooling unit" that makes it easier for people to share resources and labors, "a place where members who may not have been biologically related" might "contribute their various incomes" and thereby increase their "individual chances for survival."[16] Households can share meal preparation, gardens, heat, rent, internet service, etc., and have been structured in many ways that include multiple generations, children from other families, boarders renting rooms, college roommates, communes and religious communities, and so on. Prior to industrialized capitalism, both women and men did most of their labor for the household. These "were not categorically distinct activities," but industrialization put men's labor outside the home and women's inside the home, which "contributed to the belief that there existed two separate spheres of activity," and this formalized "a rigid and hierarchical gendered division of labor."[17] White bourgeois women were expected to stay at home and do domestic work for free, and soon this type of work became the marker of femininity itself, "associated with domesticity, caregiving, physical weakness and dependence, and this ideology shaped both the jobs women could access and the wage they were paid."[18] Black women also did domestic work, often both for their own families (for free) and for other families (for a low wage). Therefore, the context of industrialization was the lynchpin in defining what we now think of as the nuclear family and the hegemonic form of a household. These gendered roles within the household began to be written into the rules of companies and into the laws of the U.S. government in the first half of the twentieth century. For instance, the Ford Motor Company famously hired men who were heterosexual, married, and whose partners were required to be housewives; the company even hired sociologists to perform random drop-ins at workers' houses to ensure that the wives were keeping house properly, and if there was not a proper gendered division of labor, the male worker could be fired. The Ford Motor Company deemed this keeping their workers in "good moral standing."[19] At the same time, the U.S. government was creating legislation that "reinforced women's roles as mothers and wives."[20] During the 1930s, President Franklin D. Roosevelt's New Deal, although applauded as positive for the working class, also enforced gendered and racial hierarchies. Married women were denied and fired from jobs (since the government believed that women ought to be dependent upon their husbands' wages). Furthermore, Social Security did not cover agricultural and domestic workers, which disproportionately affected workers of color.

Let us denaturalize the current understanding of family. While the bourgeois, patriarchal, nuclear family is believed to be the best way to raise children, it has never been made clear what this means or if it is true. We have little to lose in trying other modes of family and support. For the past 300 years, the current understanding of marriage and family has been an "over program" that structures the way people live. This is why our culture has celebrations and rituals to buttress it. Our first step in moving past it into the future is to realize that no, family has not "been around since the dawn of time" in its current form, nor has it always been accepted as the best or only way to organize human society and households. A specific economic and political system defined the familial household in that way. There is no reason that we cannot change that definition by imagining different communal households with origins in our present moment.

QUESTIONING MARRIAGE AND HETERONORMATIVITY

Why uphold the patriarchal nuclear family as the ideal, especially since most people cannot (or do not want to) achieve it? For feminists like myself, this is not a desirable ideal, for it is based on pernicious beliefs about gender essentialism. Behind it is an underlying assumption that sexuality should be monogamous, lifelong, and based on two people of different gender roles. One of its building blocks is the concept of the foundational importance of blood (or the "gene fetish"[21]) and the related idea that children are best taught, socialized, and raised in the milieu of a patriarchal, nuclear family. We should be asking: Raised toward *what?* But let us first discuss marriage as the presumed norm.

Heteronormative marriage continues to hold sway, even among people who do not fit neatly within its traditional boundaries and among people whom this "ideal structure" has harmed or rejected. The figure of it acts as a normalizing and disciplining structure. Although there may have been some broadening of what that structure can accept, "the reality of gendered and sexualized lives after the sexual revolution is not one of genuine emancipation," as heteronormativity continues to "shape acceptable sexual practices" including "nonmarital heterosexual relations, same-sex couples, and some degree of trans rights."[22] In the case of marriage, rarely has an institution been so resilient in the face of its own utter failure. Perhaps only capitalism itself enjoys such unearned resiliency.

The main failure of marriage is that it is based upon the ownership of women. I have argued that capitalism organized marriage and the family in specific ways, and that capitalism needed to solidify the gender hierarchy. However, we should not mistake this to mean that there was no sexism prior to capitalism. The ownership of women predates capitalism by millennia; Thorstein Veblen argued that the ownership of women was in fact the first form of ownership in human society.[23] (Some class reductionist Marxists try to argue that sexism exists *because* of capitalism, which is nonsense. Sexism exists and existed before, within, and outside of capitalism.) The vestiges of this ownership relation linger today when a father "gives" the bride to the husband, when the bride wears white to signify that no other man has "had" her, when women change their last names in marriage to reflect their new owners, and the change from Miss to Mrs. Many families still practice these rituals and consider them romantic ceremonial gestures.

Heteronormativity continues to naturalize specific ways of living, "framing particular household forms and divisions of labor as products of human nature and as necessary foundations of a healthy human society across time."[24] Given that we live in a patriarchal society, it seems unlikely that there can be sexual or romantic relationships between women and men based on equality. Desires are never pure or merely an instinctual or physical drive. A *drive* (material, physical force) is always a *desire* (understood through culture), as psychoanalysts say. So, if a man is sexually attracted to a woman, we as philosophers should ask why.

What about womanhood is appealing and desirable to a man? Given that femininity (particularly White femininity) has been constructed as passive, childlike, and emotional, we might ask if heterosexual men are turned on by fragility. Is it ever really possible to be attracted to a woman without those constructions? The same would be true in the reverse: Why is a heterosexual woman attracted to a man? Is it sexual attraction, or is it an attraction to power, money, success, and authority that could protect her from a harsh world? Given that the feminine is constructed as desiring commitment and protection rather than sex, is it ever possible to get away from these constructions? We can ask critical questions of these constructions, we can play with them, read our scripts differently (perhaps ironically), as Judith Butler says, but there is no way to have sexual desire without moving through (consciously or not) these oppressive structures of the feminine and masculine categories. To believe that one's sexual desire is purely "natural" is to be stuck in ideology both unconscious and pernicious. It is only when heterosexual people begin to ask critical questions of their own desires, why they have them, where they come from, how they might be sexually attracted to different persons or practices in the future, etc., that something like an ethical heterosexuality may become possible. And, frankly, to ask those questions is to already escape heteronormativity and be on the path of queerness, even if one is sexually attracted to the opposite gender.

My analysis of the problems with heterosexuality is in line with that of Shulamith Firestone in the 1970s. Like Simone de Beauvoir, Firestone believes that there can never be healthy love between men and women where the political context around them is unequal. And it *is* unequal. When there has not been an equal number of women political leaders of the United States (nor even one president), when women CEOs, board chairs, and company presidents are still rare, when women still do not earn the same wage as men and still do the vast majority of housework, when women (especially women of color) still do the majority of low-paying service work, when the majority of recognized artists and film directors are men, and when rape, sexual assault, and harassment are crimes predominantly perpetrated by men against women and feminine people, it is clear that the gender binary still exists, and one side of that binary has far less political and economic power, cultural influence, and freedom for self-determination than the other. Things have improved slightly since Beauvoir and Firestone proclaimed heterosexuality as bad for women, but only slightly. And some things are worse. Many people believe that the problem is fixed, that "gender is over," or that economic class is the superstructure. We cannot fix what we refuse to see. As Firestone says at the beginning of *The Dialectic of Sex*, "Sex class is so deep as to be invisible."[25]

Like Beauvoir, Firestone argues that love is a very different thing for women and men: "woman needs love, first for its natural enriching function, and second, for social and economic reasons which have nothing to do with love."[26] Since women are rarely granted recognition for their brilliance and work in the broader world, they tend to seek identity and recognition through love and the private household. That is, "women must have love not only for healthy reasons but actually to validate their existence."[27] Love is too important for heterosexual women, and so they can never be spontaneous, joyous, and free in love; there is always some calculation. Men complain that women "seldom love a man for his individual traits but rather for what he has to offer (his class), that they are calculating, that they use sex to gain other ends, etc."[28] This is perhaps true, but it is to be expected in heterosexuality, where one side has more power than the other.

Many people understand "rape culture" to be inexplicably tied to heteronormativity. After all, "the everyday taken-for-granted normative forms of heterosexuality work as a cultural scaffolding for rape."[29] This is because sex conceptualized under patriarchy is based on a gendered norm of "women's passive acquiescing (a)sexuality and men's forthright, urgent pursuit of sexual 'release.'"[30] In "Body Politics: The Social Reproduction of Sexualities," Alan Sears claims that "Sexual assault is not the product of a few men gone rogue; it is systemic and indeed normalized."[31] In other words, rape is not the opposite of heteronormativity, it is an extreme case of our normative gender relations. Sears rightly critiques the solutions to rape as couched in language about "consent." The fact that our sexuality is in this place shows how very deep the problem is, even when we come up with "solutions" for the violence of patriarchy. He writes, "The 'naturally' superior, active, and sexually aggressive male makes an initiative, or offers a contract, to which a 'naturally' subordinate, passive woman 'consents.' . . . An egalitarian sexual relationship cannot rest on this basis; it cannot be grounded in 'consent.'"[32] The fact that our society considers consent the moral baseline for healthy sexuality is unacceptable.

Heteronormativity is unfulfilling for men because they can never be sure of being fully loved as themselves and not as mere providers or means to the end of capital, and it is unfulfilling for women because their emotional and personal freedom is constantly narrowed, thwarted, and frustrated. Heteronormativity can never be the ethical-political context for building healthy relations with a community or family, or caring for young people, or personal and societal maturation. For women in our patriarchal society, Firestone writes, there is "no other way to handle their frustration because there *is* no way to handle it, *short of revolution*."[33] If we want love and sexuality that is enriching for all, let us work toward a queer revolution.

WHAT IS A CHILD?

Just as we must denaturalize our conception of heterosexuality, we must do the same with the concept of the child. The concept of "childhood" was instituted in particular times for particular reasons and changes to suit the demands of the society.

Traditionally, the main purpose of marriage was to produce children. In many times and places, one of the wife's duties has been to create genetic progeny (especially male heirs) for the husband and his name. King Henry VIII of England famously had six wives, two of whom he ordered beheaded and two of whom he divorced (founding an entirely new Church in opposition to Catholicism in order to do so!) because they could not give him sons as heirs. If the purpose of obtaining a wife is to reproduce your genes, it follows that it is legitimate to replace your wife if she has not produced the goods.

Henry VIII lived in sixteenth-century England, but in a related case in 2004, a husband in the United Kingdom expected that his wife would produce genetic children for him, but she was not getting pregnant "and they could not afford a surrogate in the UK."[34] After months of searching for a surrogate and not finding one that they could afford, in the words of the surrogacy doctor (who tellingly uses the term "girl" to describe the wife), "the girl's *mother*, that is the *grandmother*, delivered twins for the daughter. And when I saw the end result, I was *really happy!* Because the husband was ready to divorce that girl" and "the husband 'wanted his wife's genes or was ready to throw her out.'"[35] Why support keeping this marriage together? Is it based on "love" and "commitment," as so many defenders of marriage claim, or is it based upon the wife's ability to provide progeny for the husband? The gene fetish carries forth in couples both heterosexual and homosexual, who insist that having genetic progeny be part of their family plan. This sheds light on what people (often unconsciously) think a family really is. If a family at its core were about love, commitment, and caring for the vulnerable, including children, then there would not be this obsession with genetic progeny. The fact that millions of people spend millions of dollars (through infertility treatments, egg freezing, surrogacy, etc.) in order to replicate the patriarchal notion of the biological nuclear family shows that the modern family is still about the creation of genetic progeny. We have progressed since Henry VIII in some respects, but our continuing obsession with genetic progeny stems from the same source.

Firestone insists that the root of women's oppression is pregnancy, that biological reality is socially constructed in line with political contexts. She writes that "there is value in understanding the relativity of the oppression; though it has been a fundamental human condition, it has appeared to differing degrees in different forms."[36] Grasping this relativity leads us to rethink what we conceptualize as the patriarchal nuclear family, which, Firestone reminds us, "has a relatively short history, roughly from the fourteenth century on" and then again changed drastically at the birth of industrialization and capitalism.[37]

Firestone impressively compares the status of children in the Middle Ages, the Victorian Age, and the 1970s. "In the Middle Ages there was no such thing as childhood,"[38] she writes. The concept of children as distinct from adults was not in people's consciousness; they were small adults in apprenticeship to full adults. In fact, "there was no special vocabulary to describe them," just as there were no special games, toys, activities, schooling, or spaces just for children.[39] Children were not privately raised by their parents as they are today; the household in the Middle Ages was still patriarchal, but that household was large and not entirely based on blood relations. The family at that time was closer to the original meaning of the word: a structure with a male boss in charge of the members of household including the wife, the children, the servants, etc. As Firestone reminds us, "*famulus* means domestic slave, and *familia* is the total number of slaves belonging to one man."[40] The small adults (children) of the household were considered servants and apprentices of a type, regardless of parentage. Firestone describes how "the child was wetnursed by a stranger, and thereafter sent to another home" until about age 15 to serve as "an apprentice to a master." Thus "he never developed a heavy dependence on his parents" and the parents "in turn did not 'need' their children—children were certainly not doted upon."[41] They also were never segregated into child-only spaces but were integrated into the household with people of all ages and classes, some blood relatives, most not.

It was only in the seventeenth century that we started to speak of children as a special class of human beings. Toys or games made especially for children "did not appear until 1600 and were not used beyond the age of three or four."[42] Yet, times change, and "by the seventeenth century childhood as a new and fashionable concept was in."[43] According to Firestone, this is when we start to see the bourgeois, child-centered family, when special costumes, distinct games, and portraits of wealthy children began to appear. Even then, there was a gender division in childhood: Girls were often married off around the time of puberty, whereas bourgeois boys generally had a long youth filled with games, sports, schooling and/or labor apprenticeships, and were not expected to marry until their 20s, 30s, or later. Childhood has never been for all children, even in bourgeois families.

(Furthermore, race, class, and capitalism collide to create the notion that some humans have a childhood with distinct parameters and protections. Today, immigrant and refugee children in detention camps in the U.S. are not protected. Juvenile detention is more often for White children, and children of color are more often treated as adults in the criminal justice system. Even in the twenty-first century, childhood is not for all children.)

When games and toys started being invented for children, they were seen as *only* for children, and adults stopped playing. Our earlier section on Winnicott (see chapter 2) demonstrated that one of the reasons adults may not think critically and expansively is that they lose their sense of play. Losing one's sense of play has nothing to do with the years one has lived. Our reading of

Firestone is in line with our earlier position that who plays and who does not play is socially constructed. Adults should play! Play encourages a sense of possibility and wonder. New worlds, new rules, and new personas are possible in games and play. One may start to see that they could be a different type of person, that the world, too, could be otherwise than it is, which is the basis of all critical theory. As it is, however, we think of play as something for a particular class of people, for a limited time only.

The new conception of the family that arose in the 16th and 17th centuries and accelerated in the 18th was a self-enclosed unit with certain people who were considered fully dependent on the parents due to their weakness and lack of abilities and intelligence. Whereas young people in earlier centuries were integrated in the household and thought capable of learning and doing many things, new children (at least the idealized children of the bourgeois classes) had to be protected and doted upon, everything done for them. Then as now, "we underestimate the capabilities of children."[44] The same is true of the White women in the family, who were grouped together with children as "pure" and "innocent." White women and children were under the auspices of "cute," denoting their naïve lack of intelligence, their object appearance status, and their dependence on men who were more rational and thus in a better position to make choices for them. (The anti-abortion movement is a modern example of this lingering belief that women are not capable or rational enough to make their own life choices. The government, judges, philosophers, legislators, and others need to think *for* them. The 24-hour waiting period required to obtain an abortion in some U.S. states is indicative of this, as if women cannot make choices without official institutional assistance.) Protection of women and children so often means defining them as incompetent. Making someone dependent upon you is often what creates their weakness, not the other way around.

Concurrently with the development of the modern conception of the nuclear family, Firestone writes, "the oppression of women and children was increasingly intertwined":[45]

> The development of the modern family meant the breakdown of a large, integrated society into small, self-centered units. The child of these units now became important; for he was the product of that unit, the reason for its maintenance. It became desirable to keep one's children at home for as long as possible to bind them psychologically, financially, and emotionally to the family unit until such time as they were ready to create a new family unit.[46]

And so it goes. Distinct little units reproduce themselves along with patriarchal ideology, blood and gene fetishes, the oppression of women, and the increasing lack of freedom for children. Today, many bourgeois children are scheduled or supervised nearly every minute of the day. They are seen as precious commodities of the nuclear family who must be protected, nurtured, and doted upon at every turn. The obsessive nurturing and protection of children is not doing them or their caregivers any favors in terms of the work we all must do to mature into well-rounded human beings.

An obvious positive consequence of the changing status of the child is that in the early 20th century, questions arose regarding the exploitation of child labor. Before this time, it was common for children to work long hours in or outside the home. It would take several centuries after the development of the concept of "childhood" to outlaw child labor, and even then, most laws did not cover all children but focused on bourgeois children, while poor children, immigrant children, children of color, and rural children on farms were not (and are not) so protected. On the negative side, however, to believe that children require constant care and entertainment means that someone must do all that work. Within the patriarchal family, it fell to the proletariats of the family, the women and servants. With the invention of these new roles and duties, the nuclear family required even more power to be instituted in its foundation.

WHAT IS SOCIAL REPRODUCTION THEORY?

The current nuclear family has its roots in the birth of capitalism and the industrial age. Many contemporary Marxist feminists use the phrase "social reproduction theory" to talk about how women's place in society was strictly defined and demoted during the industrial age. Although we shall not forget that sexism exists in many forms and under many types of economy, not just under capitalism, it is helpful to look at the social reproduction theorists' views to note the ways in which capitalism has defined roles within the family. I certainly do not believe that moving toward a communist economy would remedy all sexism in its various guises and modalities across sexuality, race, and different cultures, for I agree with Firestone that sexism is the first form of oppressive class structure and that, if anything, capitalism learns its hierarchal models from sex class, not the other way around. This is why any revolution that seeks to squash hierarchical oppression must always fight on many fronts, e.g., sex, race, ability, sexuality, species, *and* class. Fighting on only one front will not win the war.

Social reproduction theory attempts to fight from two bases, economic class and sex class, so it could be helpful to us in understanding and redefining family. Nancy Fraser writes in "Crisis of Care? On the Social-Reproductive Contradictions of Contemporary Capitalism" that within capitalism, since "at least the industrial era," society began to separate "the work of social reproduction" from the work of "economic production" and associated "the first with women and the second with men."[47] According to most theorists in the field, social reproduction includes activities such as birthing and caring for children, cleaning and making serene living spaces, creating, mending, and laundering clothing, shopping for food and planning and cooking meals, and providing sexual and emotional labor for family members. Other theorists also include activities such as caring for and building bonds with neighbors and friends, engaging in acts of community and culture building, caring for the elderly and the disabled, teaching and storytelling, organizing community celebrations and parties, creating and stimulating arts and crafts, and many more. Much of this work is unpaid, for social reproduction is the work that makes "economic work" possible. In the introduction to *Social Reproduction Theory: Remapping Class, Recentering Oppression*, Tithi Bhattacharya gestures toward broadening social reproduction "to include processes lying outside this worker's household" like the education the worker received, the public transportation or streets and highways that help her get to work, or the "public parks and libraries that provide recreation so that she can be regenerated" to go to work again.[48] However, when most theorists write about social reproduction, it is clear that they speak primarily of work within the private household, caring for one's "own" family. Some call these activities affective labor, emotional labor, care work, or support work.

A division between social reproduction and economic production assumes that the former need not be paid because such activities are done in the "coin of 'love' and 'virtue,'" whereas productive work is paid in money.[49] Within capitalism, money is power, and women generally have less of both. Thus, those who do social reproductive work rather than productive work "are structurally subordinate."[50] As Silvia Federici rightly maintains, "Violence has always been present as a subtext, a possibility, in the nuclear family, because men, through their wages, have been given the power to supervise women's unpaid domestic labor, to use women as their servants, and to punish their refusal to work."[51] Until the 18th century, courts put women on trial for disagreeing with their husbands (or merely talking too much) and might force a disagreeable woman to wear a cage around her head with a spiked bit over her tongue; she had to wear this cage around town as she did her servant duties, acting as a living warning to other women.[52] It is only very recently that domestic assault and rape within marriage have been recognized as crimes,[53] for these are the logical consequences if wives are seen as unpaid servants whose "job" is to support and care for their husbands: If she does not do her job, she must be disciplined.

Therefore, in social reproduction theory, the labor of the world is split into two categories, economically productive and socially productive, and those who do the latter (mostly women) will necessarily be lower in the hierarchy than those who do the former. Social reproduction theorists differ in the remedies to this, but the move to communism is thought to wipe out the distinction between the two forms of labor and thus free women from the secondary status of serving economic producers. However, in contemporary capitalism, only in the wealthiest families do women perform only social reproduction. The economy being what it is, it requires almost everyone to be in the game of economic production. In addition to domestic duties, women must also bring home enough money to support themselves and their families, and even then, women still do the lion's share of socially productive labor at home and at work.

A CRITIQUE OF SOCIAL REPRODUCTION THEORY

Play has been a consistent theme in our exploration of the concept of maturity. From Winnicott to Marcuse to Firestone to social reproduction theory, psychoanalysts, Marxists, and feminists all seem to emphasize the importance of play. Depending on the context (class, culture, era), children may have more or less time for non-capitalist activities like play, the activities that can "transform their worlds in ways that allow new meanings and possibilities to flourish" and engage the senses while bringing "imagination and concrete interactions with the environment together."[54] Play is different from work, not necessarily in the activity itself (for instance, one could grow and pick tomatoes from the garden as an act of play or an act of work), but rather in the freedom and expression of the subject. Both players and workers engage with and transform the environment, but in play, the imagination and senses are freer to glean the possible. Or, in Susan Ferguson's words, play, unlike work, is "often pleasurable and/or aimed at creating something better."[55]

For the most part, at least in bourgeois homes, children are freed from having to do productive/economic work to sustain their lives. In the early stages of childhood, one's parents or guardians take care of that. However, there is a gradual turning of children into productive and/or social reproductive workers as they age. Furthermore, social reproduction theorists posit that it is mostly women who do the labor of raising children, of "reproducing" the society into workers of the next generation. In "Children, Childhood and Capitalism: A Social Reproduction Perspective," Ferguson writes, "childhood under capitalism is incontrovertibly the space and time in which such a transformation is set in motion" because, over time, children "take increasing responsibility for their own social reproduction."[56] Children must be molded into the social reality that they face once they are responsible for their own productive and/or socially reproductive lives; they "must learn their way into those capitalist subjectivities."[57] Thus, "raising" children is about forming and deforming interests, proclivities, and senses of duty, or, in other words, carving out subjectivities. As "responsible" parents and guardians are under pressure to raise children as the future supply of labor power for the capitalist machine, they prepare children for lives of alienation. This means narrowing the child's interests from what is *possible* to what *is.*

This is a perfect system for the capitalists: The more children we have and the more the family is privatized, the more we all have to buckle under. Family structure becomes a major disciplinary structure. All wider social support is taken away, for the family is a private venture. We are convinced that we will not be fulfilled in life unless we get married and have babies. And our kids will grow up to be just like us and repeat the cycle.

But it need not be this way. First, let us develop a model for the creation of family and the development of children that is not based on privatization, individualism, and ownership, all facets of capitalism, but on communities of care and responsibility to one another. Small communities of love and attachment can be formed, but they need not have anything to do with marriage, children, or genetics. As Lewis writes, "Let us hold one another hospitably, explode notions of hereditary parentage, and multiply real, loving solidarities. Let us build a care commune based on comradeship, a world sustained by kith and kind more than by kin."[58]

Second, we must recognize that "private" decisions do not happen in a vacuum. What one does affects all living things. In my view, a major problem with the social reproduction theory is that it is stuck in another era. We live in a time of climate catastrophe, of massive forest fires sweeping Australia, Brazil, and California, of polar ice caps melting, of droughts and polluted waters, of global pandemics. When discussing family and life plans, so few people take into serious consideration the effect that their "private" family choices have on the planet. This is another aspect of casting family as a private venture: It is wreaking havoc on the environment. Humans have far overstepped any kind of species allotment for space and resources on this planet. In addition, our arrogance and self-absorption mean that we have assumed the right to kill and use nonhuman animals as we please. Even when most people do speak about "protecting the environment," they quickly follow it with phrases like "for our grandchildren" and "for the next generation." If life should be preserved, it must be preserved for all species, all of our Earth kin.

Therein lies the problem: Social reproduction theorists define social reproduction as primarily (but not only) birthing and caring for human children and reproducing workers. This idea might have made sense in Marx's time, but in our time it is drastically narrow. More human beings on the planet is decidedly not what we need in order for our species and other species to persist. In fact, we need the opposite.

In this way, "social reproduction" should be redefined as those actions that make the planet livable for the future of all Earth kin, reproducing the possibilities and foundations for living. Birthing biological babies and caring for them does not always fulfill that definition. Philosophy and theory need to catch up to the material reality of our world. Being a vegan activist, a climate justice activist, a water protector, a rainforest protector, an activist on behalf of free access to birth control and abortion—these are the kinds of practices that will help our world continue and "reproduce" the conditions for living and working.

NEW CONCEPTUALIZATIONS OF KIN

Let us consider the primates who, when they know the environment (food, shelter, weather) is unstable, choose to birth fewer babies. Many of the females in a primate clan will not birth babies but will instead adopt and care for the rare few babies that are born. Group members care for the vulnerable who are not necessarily their blood relatives. They become a commune of cooperative care. While nature is not in and of itself a moral good, we must use critical theory in order to estimate which acts are good, and in the above example, the members of the primate clan have learned how to do what is best for the justice and continued existence of the whole. We need to learn how to do that, too, because right now, we are taking our own species and many others down with us.

Donna Haraway and I are comrades on this latter issue. In *Staying with the Trouble: Making Kin in the Chthulucene*, she writes that the slogan for our time should be "Make kin, not babies!" By kin, she means learning to "become-with," being in curious and open relations with members of our species and other species. We need to recognize them as our kin, "we need to make-with—become-with, compose-with—the earth-bound."[59] As Haraway explains,

> My purpose is to make "kin" mean something other/more than entities tied by ancestry or genealogy. . . . All earthlings are kin in the deepest sense, and it is past time to practice better care of kinds-as-assemblages (not species one at a time). Kin is an assembling sort of work. All critters share a common "flesh," laterally, semiotically, and genealogically. Ancestors turn out to be very interesting strangers . . . So, make kin, not babies! It matters how kin generate kin.[60]

Haraway and I are cognizant of the racist, classist, and ableist history surrounding the concept of "population control," the ways in which women of color, poor people, incarcerated people, and disabled people have been involuntarily sterilized, the histories of indigenous and Native peoples whose children were stolen from them. Neither of us use the phrase "population control," for we do not believe in imposing control from outside or above; rather, we want a change of consciousness, a new understanding of our desires, our gendered senses of self, and our definition of kin.

In challenging the ideal of the biological family, Haraway traces the entwined history of racism and sexism in America, a hierarchical society fixated on order and progress. At the founding of the country, strict hierarchies of gender were established within the family, of families within society, and of societies as nations, in terms of which nations or peoples were more "civilized" than others. The entire hierarchy is, of course, topped by the White/European, heterosexual, bourgeois, Christian, biological nuclear family. The very fact that colonization could happen was premised upon this hierarchy, for how else could colonizers take over lands and peoples, all the while telling themselves and others that they were serving "progress"? As these types of hierarchy drive colonization, so they organize the biological family, in which a male head of the household gives his name and a civilizing legitimacy to the rest of the members. Haraway writes, "For many in the first decades of the twentieth century, race mixing was a venereal disease of the social body producing doomed progeny whose reproductive issue was as tainted as that of lesbians, sodomites, Jews, overeducated women, prostitutes, criminals, masturbators, or alcoholics," all understood within the "commodious discourse of eugenics."[61] Haraway points out that even when we as a culture began to question racism as a hierarchy, the hierarchical way of thinking itself was never completely questioned. She cites work from Charlotte Perkins Gilman and W.E.B. Du Bois, who reject the biologism of racism but accept it in understanding notions of the family, civilizations, and the "childhood and maturity of collective human groups called races."[62] We see here that notions of blood as kinship and racism are related.

Only a few decades later came the sway of "the species-defining sharing way of life, rooted in hunting and in the heterosexual nuclear family,"[63] which is where we get the myths of Man-as-Hunter and Woman-as-Gatherer. We moved away from the belief in a natural hierarchy of races to a "universal race" of the species, but the hierarchy and sexism of the family still lingers. Haraway writes, "The antiracist universals of the evolutionary drama scripted according to the humanist doctrines" nonetheless "left in place the durable essentials of the sexual division of labor, male-headed heterosexual families and child-laden females."[64] Like Haraway, I reject the "numbing and hegemonic sameness" of the supposed "universal way of life."[65] If it is universally human to be collected up into "the reproductive heterosexual nuclear family," then a whole lot of us are less than human, because "what's not collected in a reproductive family story does not finally count as human."[66] Philosophers must move past this obsession with what is human, the Anthropos, "the upward-looking one."[67]

Many environmental philosophers deem our current epoch the "Anthropocene." Anna Tsing writes that this begins with geologists, who use the term to describe "the epoch in which human disturbance outranks other geological forces."[68] "Without planning or intention, humans have made a mess of our planet," she writes in *The Mushroom at the End of the World: On the Possibility of Life in Capitalist Ruins*. However, Tsing is quick to rightly point out that this is not a result of our "species biology" but of capitalism, "a technique of alienation that turns both humans and other beings into resources."[69] Fewer humans on the planet would do less damage. As discussed in the first chapter, Tsing argues that precarity (of our species and others) is the state of our world, a "condition of being vulnerable" in "a world without teleology."[70] We live in a frightening indeterminacy where, at least at some level, we all know that "there might not be a collective happy ending."[71]

Thinking with Tsing, Haraway speaks of how our present world lacks spaces of refuge: "Perhaps the outrage meriting a name like Anthropocene is about the destruction of places and times of refuge for people and other critters,"[72] for "Right now, the earth is full of refugees, human and not, without refuge."[73] Haraway is a scientist, a biologist, so she keeps a close eye on the material shifts of the planet and its life. Numbers matter. She notes that by the end of the century, there will likely be 11 billion human beings, adding that "rapid anthropogenic climate change shows that 7–11 billion human beings make demands that cannot be borne without immense damage to human and nonhuman beings across the earth."[74] She concludes: "The edge of extinction is not just a metaphor; system collapse is not a thriller. Ask any refugee of any species."[75]

Because of the racist, ableist, and classist histories of discussions surrounding human population, Haraway writes endnotes to her chapter that are nearly as long as the chapter itself, carefully unwrapping her points with arguments both scientific (data-driven) and philosophical (justice-driven). I imagine that she has been called out many times for daring to state that we urgently need to lower the birth rate of the human species. Yet we cannot shirk the duty of bringing up this topic because it is difficult. Such "denial will not serve us," Haraway remarks.[76] Feminists are ideally placed to continue this discussion because we have long resisted essentialism, the tie between sex and gender, between womanhood and motherhood. We resist the patriarchal ideology that tells women that becoming pregnant is a necessary aspect of a fulfilling feminine life. Let us be activists and provocateurs toward different "cultural expectations" and a "new normal" in line with global species diversity and flourishing.[77]

Deflection will kill us all, humans and non-humans. "These issues demand difficult, unrelenting work" such as finding ways to "celebrate low birth rates" and ways to live "flourishing and generous lives . . . without making more babies," which is urgently and especially needed in "high consumption" regions.[78] We should lobby for free, safe, and easily accessible vasectomies, birth control, and abortion health care. Haraway also speaks of creating celebrations and honors for those who do the work of preserving the planet, much as we have celebrations now for those who do the opposite. We should invent rituals for people choosing not to birth biological children but who practice other forms of kinship-making, caring for kin across generations, race, gender, sexuality, and species.

Even some of those who "believe" in global warming and agree that the human species is using too many earthly resources will idly point the finger at large systems or corporations without changing their own lives. Their traditional commitments and ways of living are "too deep to allow rethinking and refeeling."[79] But "blaming Capitalism, Imperialism, Neoliberalism, Modernization or some other 'not us' for ongoing destruction webbed with human numbers will not work either."[80] Rather, let us act in accordance with our values. For instance, veganism is a political movement that seeks to change the way all humans use resources like water and soil, changing the mindset that our species has some "right" to use and exploit the lives and bodies of other species. Let us take up less space and resources on the planet so that others (including other species) may have their own flourishing lives. Let us promote veganism and fight capitalism at the same time!

Haraway states unambiguously:

> I am sick to death of bonding through kinship and "the family," and I long for models of solidarity and human unity and difference rooted in friendship, work, partially shared purposes, intractable collective pain, inescapable mortality, and persistent hope. It is time to theorize an "unfamiliar" unconscious, a different primal scene, where everything does not stem from the dramas of identity and reproduction. Ties through blood—including blood recast in the coin of genes and information—have been bloody enough already.[81]

My favorite line from Sophie Lewis's book *Full Surrogacy Now* is "We are the makers of one another."[82] I began this project of political maturity precisely because each of us is the maker of one another and we help each other to expand or to stagnate. This "making" is not optional—it is an ethical-political responsibility. It will be challenging for us to imagine and practice new modes of kinship. This is especially true because as "adults," we are not accustomed to thinking in imaginative ways, having left play behind long ago. But this work is urgent and must be accomplished not only because justice calls for the elimination of hierarchies (sex, class, race, sexualities) but because we must stop reproducing the lifeways of the generations before us. Their world is not our world. Let us explore our consciousness in discussions with others and seek out that which serves the future liberation of all. We succeed as Earth kin or we, as humans, fail us all.

NOTES

1. Shulamith Firestone, *The Dialectic of Sex: The Case for Feminist Revolution* (New York: Macmillan, 1970), 67. Quoted with permission of Macmillan Publishers.

2. Firestone, *The Dialectic of the Sex*, 12.

3. Firestone, *The Dialectic of the Sex*, 12.

4. Firestone, *The Dialectic of the Sex*, 12.

5. Emily Fitzgibbons Shafer, "Hillary Rodham Versus Hillary Clinton: Consequences of Surname Choice in Marriage," *Gender Issues* 34 (2017): 316–32, https://doi.org/10.1007/s12147-016-9182-5.

6. Nina Totenberg and Sarah McCammon, "Supreme Court Overturns Roe v. Wade, Ending Right to Abortion Upheld for Decades," *All Things Considered*, NPR, June 24, 2022, https://www.npr.org/2022/06/24/1102305878/supreme-court-abortion-roe-v-wade-decision-overturn.

7. Sophie Lewis, *Full Surrogacy Now: Feminism Against Family* (London: Verso Books, 2021), 116.

8. Silvia Federici, *Caliban and the Witch: Women, the Body and Primitive Accumulation* (New York: Autonomedia, 2004), 204.

9. Federici, *Caliban and the Witch*, 204.

10. Federici, *Caliban and the Witch*, 203.

11. Lewis, *Full Surrogacy Now*, 17.

12. Silvia Federici, *Witches, Witch-Hunting, and Women* (San Francisco: PM Press, 2018), 54.

13. Federici, *Witches, Witch-Hunting, and Women*, 54.

14. Federici, *Witches, Witch-Hunting, and Women*, 51.

15. Field, Connie, dir. The Life and Times of Rosie the Riveter. 1980; Berkeley, CA: Clarity Films, 2014. DVD.

16. Salar Mohandesi and Emma Teitelman, "Without Reserves," in *Social Reproduction Theory: Remapping Class, Recentering Oppression*, ed. Tithi Bhattacharya (London: Pluto Press, 2017), 40.

17. Mohandesi and Teitelman, "Without Reserves," 42–43.

18. Mohandesi and Teitelman, "Without Reserves," 44.

19. Mohandesi and Teitelman, "Without Reserves," 49.

20. Mohandesi and Teitelman, "Without Reserves," 50.

21. Lewis, *Full Surrogacy Now*, 20.

22. Alan Sears, "Body Politics: The Social Reproduction of Sexualities," in *Social Reproduction Theory: Remapping Class, Recentering Oppression*, ed. Tithi Bhattacharya (London: Pluto Press, 2017), 171.

23. Thorstein Veblen, *The Theory of the Leisure Class: An Economic Study of Institutions* (New York: The Macmillan Company, 1912).

24. Sears, "Body Politics," 172.

25. Firestone, *The Dialectic of Sex*, 3.

26. Firestone, *The Dialectic of Sex*, 130.

27. Firestone, *The Dialectic of Sex*, 124.

28. Firestone, *The Dialectic of Sex*, 125–26.

29. Nicola Gavey, *Just Sex? The Cultural Scaffolding of Rape* (New York: Routledge, 2019), 2.
30. Sears, "Body Politics," 184.
31. Sears, "Body Politics," 184.
32. Sears, "Body Politics," 188.
33. Firestone, *The Dialectic of Sex*, 61.
34. Lewis, *Full Surrogacy Now*, 105.
35. Lewis, *Full Surrogacy Now*, 105.
36. Firestone, *The Dialectic of Sex*, 67.
37. Firestone, *The Dialectic of Sex*, 67.
38. Firestone, *The Dialectic of Sex*, 68.
39. Firestone, *The Dialectic of Sex*, 69.
40. Firestone, *The Dialectic of Sex*, 67.
41. Firestone, *The Dialectic of Sex*, 69.
42. Firestone, *The Dialectic of Sex*, 70.
43. Firestone, *The Dialectic of Sex*, 71.
44. Firestone, *The Dialectic of Sex*, 75.
45. Firestone, *The Dialectic of Sex*, 76.
46. Firestone, *The Dialectic of Sex*, 77.
47. Nancy Fraser, "Crisis of Care? On the Social-Reproductive Contradictions of Contemporary Capitalism," in *Social Reproduction Theory: Remapping Class, Recentering Oppression*, ed. Tithi Bhattacharya (London: Pluto Press, 2017), 23.
48. Tithi Bhattacharya, "Introduction: Mapping Social Reproduction Theory," in *Social Reproduction Theory: Remapping Class, Recentering Oppression*, ed. Tithi Bhattacharya (London: Pluto Press, 2017), 1–2.
49. Fraser, "Crisis of Care?" 23.
50. Fraser, "Crisis of Care?" 24.
51. Federici, *Witches, Witch-Hunting, and Women*, 49.
52. Federici, *Witches, Witch-Hunting, and Women*, 48.
53. Joann M. Ross, "Making Marital Rape Visible: A History of American Legal and Social Movements Criminalizing Rape in Marriage," PhD diss. (University of Nebraska-Lincoln, 2015), https://digitalcommons.unl.edu/cgi/viewcontent.cgi?article=1085&context=historydiss.
54. Susan Ferguson, "Children, Childhood and Capitalism: A Social Reproduction Perspective," in *Social Reproduction Theory: Remapping Class, Recentering Oppression*, ed. Tithi Bhattacharya (London: Pluto Press, 2017), 119.
55. Ferguson, "Children, Childhood and Capitalism," 118.
56. Ferguson, "Children, Childhood and Capitalism," 113.
57. Ferguson, "Children, Childhood and Capitalism," 114.
58. Lewis, *Full Surrogacy Now*, 26.
59. Donna Haraway, *Staying with the Trouble: Making Kin in the Chthulucene* (Durham: Duke University Press, 2016), 102.
60. Haraway, *Staying with the Trouble*, 101–2.
61. Donna Haraway, *The Haraway Reader* (New York: Routledge, 2004), 252.
62. Haraway, *The Haraway Reader*, 253.

63. Haraway, *The Haraway Reader*, 259.
64. Haraway, *The Haraway Reader*, 261.
65. Haraway, *The Haraway Reader*, 261.
66. Haraway, *The Haraway Reader*, 262–63.
67. Donna J. Haraway, *Manifestly Haraway* (Minneapolis: University of Minnesota Press, 2016), 294.
68. Anna Lowenhaupt Tsing, *The Mushroom at the End of the World: On the Possibility of Life in Capitalist Ruins* (Princeton: Princeton University Press, 2015), 19.
69. Tsing, *The Mushroom at the End of the World*, 19.
70. Tsing, *The Mushroom at the End of the World*, 20.
71. Tsing, *The Mushroom at the End of the World*, 20–21.
72. Haraway, *Staying with the Trouble*, 100.
73. Haraway, *Staying with the Trouble*, 100.
74. Haraway, *Staying with the Trouble*, 208.
75. Haraway, *Staying with the Trouble*, 102.
76. Haraway, *Staying with the Trouble*, 208.
77. Haraway, *Staying with the Trouble*, 209.
78. Haraway, *Staying with the Trouble*, 209.
79. Haraway, *Staying with the Trouble*, 208.
80. Haraway, *Staying with the Trouble*, 208.
81. Haraway, *The Haraway Reader*, 285.
82. Lewis, *Full Surrogacy Now*, 19.

Chapter Six

Maturing as Critical Openness

It may be helpful to return to Freud's ideas for a moment. As discussed in chapter 2, Freud presumes that the superego of the subject is limiting. He believes this precisely because the superego learns the norms for living "ethically" from the outside, from society; thus, a certain dichotomy is set up between the subject as the site of freedom and the society as the site of limitation. Of course, the subject is not a subject until she begins the process of negotiations with the outer world, as in our reading of Winnicott. This reading of Freud could be set in opposition to Emanuel Levinas's philosophy, in which it is the Other that frees the subject in the sense that the subject can only access transcendence through relation to the Other.[1] For Levinas, that transcendence through the Other is ethics. So, for both Freud and Levinas, we access ethics through something outside ourselves, which for Freud is constriction and for Levinas transcendence. I, however, think that the relation is rather more complex than this dichotomy suggests. Freedom and ethics may be on both sides (self and other), not on either side exclusively. It is this *either/both* relation that makes critique of social norms possible in the name of ethics. For instance, sometimes social norms make us less ethical.

A CRITIQUE OF CLOSEDNESS

As should be clear by now, my conception of ethics is always political, always concerned with power relations, and thus it is first and foremost a theory of justice. As an example, let us look at our species' relationship with non-human animals. I believe that we are socialized to be unethical in most cases. There is a famous photo of a bull near the end of a bullfight: Suffering and close to death, the bull recognizes his former caretaker in the audience, and in his vulnerability, the bull goes toward this man and cries out directly to him. The caretaker denies him help and gives him the "kiss of Judas." This story illustrates that in the heart of a human, an act of closure, an attitude of refusal, can take root. When faced with a vulnerable being asking for help, this refusal is what provokes us to say no, I will not help, for my society has taught me that I need not do so.

Levinas writes that "the face of the other person obligates the ego which, from the start—without deliberation—is responsive to the Other."[2] The form (what is physical) is different from what Levinas deems the face (the call to our ethical duty). As many of Levinas's readers have argued, since it is the form and not the face that takes on particular physical appearance (the shape of your eyes, the size of your nose, the color of your skin or fur), an individual from another species (with a different form) can be said to contain Levinas's "face." The vulnerability of life is present. In my example, the naked, suffering face of the bull has (in Levinas's words) begged me, pleaded with me "without defense or power," his "nudity an exposure unto death"—the face is "the very mortality" of the other.[3] When I turn away from the vulnerability of the other, when I refuse to respond to the call of the other, I have rejected ethics; I have the bull killed. Yet, such rejection, refusal, and turning away is our social norm. Most humans in most times and places have been brought up to cause suffering and death for those who are not human.

This kind of refusal is at the very intersection of ethics and civilization. Social norms may teach us and reassure us that we are doing an ethical thing even when we are not. In Freud's understanding of ethics, there seems to be little space for the subject to critique the so-called ethics of their society. This is the kind of cultural relativism of Epicurus, who believes that we should never do anything that would cause our neighbors to look askance at us.[4] As for me, I reject a Freudian/Epicurean civilization. How might we recognize those moments which call for ethical judgments and how might we make them? How might we judge, in my example above, that the caretaker was unethical? I agree with Levinas that our indication is the caretaker's shutting himself off from the call of the other in their moment of vulnerability. It seems to me that it is the very ideology of our civilization that often places a closed door on the path to ethical openness.

Imagine that instead of a bull, the call to ethics comes from a Syrian refugee who is asking for help from your nation. Imagine a child separated from their undocumented parents. Imagine a handcuffed Black trans woman who is being harassed by a police officer. In each of the cases, there is also a large number of Americans who have closed themselves off from caring about the suffering of that Other before them. This closure is validated and sometimes even encouraged by the way in which we are civilized. My critique does not mean that we instead be committed to a Rousseauian vision of humans born pure and ethically open, but Freud would have us believe that in following the accepted codes of our civilization, we are being ethical. Reflecting on maturing as striving to act ethically, I maintain that civilization often discourages openness and encourages us to act immaturely.

In summation, Freud puts ethics in the hands of society while Levinas puts ethics in the eyes of the Other. My view is that both are a little bit right and a little bit wrong. I side with Judith Butler, who writes in *Giving an Account of Oneself*,

> If the "I" is not at one with moral norms, this means only that the subject must deliberate upon these norms, and that part of deliberation will entail a critical understanding of their social genesis and meaning. In this sense, ethical deliberation is bound up with the operation of critique. And critique finds that it cannot go forward without a consideration of how the deliberating subject comes into being and how a deliberating subject might actually live or appropriate a set of norms.[5]

Butler emphasizes that ethics relies upon the ability to critique society. I argue that maturity also relies upon and is, in some ways, the awakening of this ability. The two cases (ethics and maturity) both require the subject to be *open* but also *critical.* Douglas Kellner's reading of Marcuse uncovers something similar to what we have been discussing:

> Uncritical thinking derives its beliefs, norms, and values from existing thought and social practices, while critical thought seeks alternative modes of thought and behavior from which it creates a standpoint of critique. Such a critical standpoint requires what Marcuse calls "negative thinking." . . . Thus grasping potentialities for freedom and happiness would make possible the negation of conditions that inhibited individuals' full development and realization.[6]

How and when in our development might we learn to practice such critique? If critique is a necessary aspect of maturing—as I argue it is—which experiences can provoke it? How might we shape a society around preparing people for this practice of critique?

AHMED ON DISORIENTATION

The movement of maturing is one of *critique* and one of *opening.* In what ways might we develop (and help others to further develop) becoming critically open? Will this be an openness toward anything and everything? Surely not. How might we make wise decisions on what to be open toward? Is being closed always a sign of immaturity? Not necessarily—it depends on what we are closed toward. Sara Ahmed's *Queer Phenomenology: Orientations,*

Objects, Others is of immense help on this theme. She explores how queer people experience disorientation in the world, as the world cannot be purely closed to them if their relationship to that world is off-kilter, oblique, and not at straight angles. The world tries to orient us in certain ways, and we find ourselves askew. An orientation that is not a tight fit to the world leaves a space where air might flow, like a door that improperly fits the door jam. As air circulates where there is no tight fit, so too can ideas. Disorientation is the result of seeking to find our way in the world and not easily finding it in the ready-made orientations toward objects. Ahmed speaks about orientations as paths well-trodden and otherwise. A path only exists because so many others have walked that way; if people stopped walking on that path, it would disappear.

To be oriented is to be turned toward the world in a certain way, a way that helps us move through the world and mature within it. In the normative definition of maturity critiqued throughout this book, one is defined as mature to the degree that one is on and in alignment with a well-trodden path; that is, normative maturing is to be oriented, not disoriented. But, as should be clear by now, my understanding of maturity is nearly the opposite of this normative view. Rather than looking for maturity in an orientation to the paths well-trodden, I find Ahmed's understanding of "disorientation" to be helpful in grasping paths toward maturity.

It is nearly impossible to live a human life that encounters no disorientation. Sickness, failures, aging, struggles with money or work, seeking love or acceptance and not finding it—most of us will experience these. But which possibilities or paths are open for us in negotiating our disorientation? Where will these paths take us? Which paths appear to which groups of people? That we may all face disorientation in life does not imply that we all experience similar varieties or degrees of disorientation. Ahmed opens her book with the question, "What difference does it make 'what' or 'who' we are oriented toward in the very direction of our desire?"[7] We do not all see the same paths, and sometimes we do not have the imagination to envision a path where we have not seen others walk it.

Ahmed further argues that "moments of disorientation are vital."[8] Yet, as she reminds us, we are sometimes undone and thrown by experiences of disorientation due to oppression—i.e., these experiences do not necessarily make us more open or help us to grow, listen, or understand others. We might be "shattered" by oppression.[9] For instance, being queer and having queer politics might involve disorientation, but disorientation in itself is not always progressive, not always "radical," according to Ahmed.[10] So why, in the face of disorientation, do some people and not others become more open? Why do some poor White people find solidarity with the poor of other racial backgrounds while others become racists?[11] Why do some unpopular and lonely men become violent incels who troll and prey on women?[12]

Ahmed writes that disorientation is "unevenly distributed"—just as queer people are disoriented in a heteronormative society, so are women in a patriarchal society and people of color in a White supremacist society.[13] By way of example, Ahmed discusses Frantz Fanon's dialectic of how a Black body becomes an "object among other objects" in the world.[14] Similarly, Simone de Beauvoir describes how a woman is turned into an object both in the eyes of men and in her own mind when she willingly takes on this alien view of herself.[15] In both cases, a subject is disoriented by the fact that she feels herself to be a subject but is expected by society to repudiate that subjectivity in order to walk the normative path of her civilization. Patriarchy demands that women be objects. White supremacy demands that Black people be objects. The demand is disorienting to one's own lived experience. Members of an oppressed group will often experience disorientation whether they want to or not. It is thrust upon them.

Many people experience disorientation, but not all of them become radical. So, what do we do with such moments of disorientation? Where do we go or, rather, where do others lead us? What are the well-worn paths before us that seem like viable options? Five people might experience a similar episode of oppression, but each of the five people may respond in different ways based on their personal and social contexts. The way we see others behave gives us clues as to how we might behave, the emotions we might be allowed to express, whether we believe that we deserve respect, whether we gauge that those near us would listen carefully in a spirit of openness and compassion, and whether opening up to others might be dangerous. All of these are weighed consciously and unconsciously when we are faced with a moment of disorientation.

In sum, we have two problems with which to struggle:

1. When people *do* experience disorientation, how might we create a context in which that disorientation leads to radical, compassionate politics, to an openness?
2. When people *do not* experience disorientation (or are able to avoid it), how might we convince them to move toward critical openness?

How might we cultivate systems and social relations that foster a culture in which instances of disorientation open us, in which our own vulnerability helps us recognize the vulnerability of others? Fostering a culture in which the virtue of open vulnerability is welcome as a sign of maturing and courage might be a useful direction to follow. Recall *The Work*, the film discussed in chapter 4, in which the men who refuse to cry are seen as weaker and as not yet ready to be open. But the hope is that with time and encouragement, and with commonly available models of vulnerability around them, they too will break open, become less closed and rigid, and move forward through the trauma that has blocked them.

BLOCKS TO CRITICAL OPENNESS

Here I discuss some possible blocks to critical openness. These blocks include patriarchy, a belief in individual autonomy, and capitalism, among others.

In *One-Dimensional Man*, Herbert Marcuse argues that under capitalism, "people recognize themselves in their commodities" and begin to identify themselves with whichever brand/color/style they buy.[16] He stresses this because of the social control that it imposes. You cannot have an identity unless you buy things, and you will work harder and longer in order to be able to afford the things that will define you. This in turn means that you may not notice alienation. Likewise, we can say that this recognition of oneself in objects puts off or suspends the subject's development. Alienation could be an impetus toward critique of one's relation to the world, for "the concept of alienation seems to become questionable when the individuals identify themselves with the existence which is imposed upon them and have in it their own development and satisfaction."[17] According to Marcuse, there can be an advanced stage of alienation wherein we are swallowed by our alienated existence and no longer recognize it; there are no more dimensions from which to judge our lives of freedom and happiness, there is only one dimension: consumption. Without alienation, the gap between *what is* and *what is possible* may not be felt. But Marcuse indicates that, from the opposite side, there could be an alienation so profound that we also do not experience that necessary gap. We then fall into stagnancy and what the existentialists characterize as immanence, to borrow from Hegel. However, although critique becomes increasingly less likely, I, like Terry Eagleton, believe that there is no ideology so deep and complete that we cannot see glimpses of the outside:

> The critique of ideology, then, presumes that nobody is ever wholly mystified. . . . If it rejects the external standpoint of Enlightenment rationality, it shares with the Enlightenment this fundamental trust in the moderately rational nature of human beings. Someone who was entirely the victim of ideological delusion would not even be able to recognize an emancipatory claim upon them; and it is because people do not cease to desire, struggle, and imagine, even in the most apparently unpropitious conditions, that the practice of political emancipation is a genuine possibility.[18]

Another issue with the question of maturity and capitalism is that capitalism rewards doing, not questioning. Indeed, one's relative success as a worker under capitalism is based on doing tasks for the wages one is offered without asking too many questions. Success by success, promotion by promotion, backslap by backslap from the boss, one learns to keep one's mouth (and mind) shut and ignore potentially disorienting philosophical questions. This disorientation would threaten not only one's livelihood but also one's lifestyle, so one learns to guard against it and pretend that one does not experience it. Normative masculinity is defined by just these kinds of movements: keeping a "stiff upper lip" in a moment of difficulty, pretending not to care, pretending not to hurt. Capitalism and masculinity are hand in glove. Capitalism is born out of hypermasculinity, and patriarchy and capitalism continue to reinforce each other. A society that encourages open maturing would need to break both.

Another possible block against critical opening is the belief in the individual's total autonomy as a self that is self-sufficient and self-creating. The dichotomy between self and collective is an invention. This kind of fictive, self-originating self is critiqued by Jodi Dean in her engagement with Sherry Turkle's work. Dean takes issue with Turkle for believing that in order to become mature, one must learn how to be by oneself first, then how to be with others in some kind of secondary movement: "[Turkle] argues that networked technologies inhibit the kind of separation necessary for maturation. . . . Young people do not learn how to be alone, how to reflect on their emotions in private."[19] To Turkle, the individual is something to be protected and defended against technology, precisely because technology creates a kind of "addiction" to social media and constant connectivity; this, according to Turkle, means that a person never matures because she is always on Facebook, Instagram, or texting others.[20] Turkle interviews many teenagers and then describes young people as "pathological"[21] and "waiting for connection, fearful of abandonment, and dependent on immediate responses from others even to have feelings."[22] Dean sums up that "For Turkle, a self that is less bounded, more expansive, less separate, more connected, is immature, at risk of loneliness" and "needs to form its identity, separate itself from others, and go through the stages of becoming an individual."[23]

Dean, criticizing Turkle's staunch individualism, takes cues from Michael Hardt and Antonio Negri when she claims that "the bourgeois individual" is the "disciplined subject of civil society, the liberal subject willing to vote in public and then return home to private domesticity."[24] That this bourgeois individual is not somehow natural or primary is the resultant belief of a society raised on the ideology that "one is born alone and one dies alone; you can rely on no one but yourself," which is "enjoined, inscribed, and technologically generated in the service of capitalism."[25] In collectivity, on the other hand, we create connections to others, their ideas, their goals, to multiplicity, and we have the chance to be more mobile, less disciplined, and not so tied to the "specific norms and constraints" that make us more controllable.[26]

Another way to look at this comes from Marcuse, who argues that liberation requires that the individual be able to distinguish the real from the possible, existence from essence. This ability in turn requires individuals to be able to think for themselves, to create ideas and judgments of their own rather than merely mimic those in the wider culture: "Thus introjection implies the existence of an inner dimension distinguished from and even antagonistic to the external exigencies—an individual consciousness and an individual unconscious *apart from* public opinion and behavior."[27] However, later in the work, Marcuse says that the capitalist demands upon us even outside of our labor have "invaded the inner space of privacy and practically eliminated the possibility of that isolation in which the individual, thrown back on himself alone, can think and question and find."[28]

Perhaps a bit like Turkle, Marcuse thinks that technological-capitalist reality has "invaded and whittled down" the private space needed for introjection, and thus the "opposition to the status quo" is "whittled down," too.[29] One important difference between Turkle and Marcuse, however, is that Marcuse does not argue that the self needs to develop *first* before encountering others, as he knows this is impossible. The pre-ideological self is pure fantasy (which is why Rousseau is wrong). From the womb, we are with and among others. There will never be a chance to completely develop oneself first and apart, as every word and representation (the symbolic order) we know puts us in relation with others, and we are only a self always already among others. The dream of "work on yourself first" (much like "love yourself first") is nonsense intellectually, politically, and practically. The point is not to escape from the influence of others but to be able to critically think about their influence and be in dialectic with them. Just as there is no dialectic without critical thought, there is no dialectic without the otherness of another's idea. Or, as Marcuse puts it, "The attainment of autonomy demands conditions in which the repressed dimensions of experience can come to life again."[30] Marcuse's conception of autonomy is not the liberal/neoliberal notion of a self by and for the self; rather, Marcuse's understanding of autonomy is of a self, always entwined with others and social relations, who needs a reserve space of consciousness with which to critique those relations. His notion of a more qualified autonomy is closer to something I might accept, but I am not convinced that we should hold on to the concept of autonomy, given its popular usage and the liberal notion of the individual that it invokes.

INVITATIONS TO OPENNESS

I propose a few ways in which the impetus toward critique and openness can be provoked. Let us call them invitations to openness, since a person cannot be forced to be critically open and neither does a certain experience guarantee openness. Throughout this work, I have stressed that no one matures by themselves. We are, each of us, responsible for not only trying to be as mature as we can but also for helping those around us to mature. And if maturity requires critique, then we need to know various ways to provoke a practice of critique. To give people a goal but no modes of reaching it is intellectually dishonest. Of course, the modes I list here are not meant to be exclusive. Edmund Husserl says of the phenomenological method that he raises the question and hopes that others will take the questions and method forward; in a similar vein, I encourage everyone to devise multiple ways to provoke critique. Here I offer some invitations to openness.

Sara Ahmed describes ways of being and thinking that are akin to queerness and can provoke disorientation; for instance, "Phenomenology is full of moments of disorientation."[31] Has it not been the goal of philosophy since Socrates—or *shouldn't* it be?—to disorient us from seeing the world in normative ways? The desire of Socratic questioning is precisely to get beyond the everyday meanings of justice, love, etc. Perhaps we should claim that phenomenology is philosophical in this way, as it expects us to be able to take a queer orientation to the world, to look at it askance instead of insisting upon clear, direct, obvious meanings.

As discussed above, a queer orientation in lived experience can be a major invitation to critique. And, as the reverse of complete autonomy, collective being is a mode of invitation into openness. Another possibility is the practice of philosophy itself, of taking a commonly held idea and holding it up for inspection. This is certainly what phenomenology does when it invites us to see the world as strange. Maurice Merleau-Ponty writes, "Reflection does not withdraw from the world" but "steps back to watch the forms of transcendence fly up like sparks from a fire; it slackens the intentional threads which attach us to the world and thus brings them to our notice" and "reveals that world as strange and paradoxical."[32]

As Husserl writes, it is not only phenomenology that does this, for this questioning of the assumed is at the heart of what philosophy is, a constant and deep reflection on the "perennial" questions rather than the narrow rationalism that animated a "European crisis."[33] He argues, "Phenomenological philosophy regards itself in its whole method as a pure outcome of the methodological intentions which already animated Greek philosophy from its beginnings" and it "demands that the phenomenologist foreswear the ideal of a philosophic system and yet as a humble worker in community with others, live for a perennial philosophy."[34] This is one of my favorite quotes about philosophy, as it reminds us that philosophy is a project demanding that questions be kept alive and that we practice within a community of others, not as elites but as humble workers of thought. I would go so far as to say that philosophy that does not provoke open critique is not philosophy.[35]

At the same time, many things that are not necessarily philosophy (movies, novels, conversations with friends) can provoke open critique of systems, too, but the problem is that these things assume openness. So we are in a chicken-and-egg situation: We need moments of disorientation in order to become more open, but we have to be open in order to recognize that our everyday life and concepts have within them the heart of the strange. Studying philosophy can certainly become an invitation to see the strange inside the everyday, but there is no guarantee.

Earlier in this section, I quoted Ahmed that "Phenomenology is full of moments of disorientation."[36] In that vein, there is a point in Husserl's work where he talks about the difference between the chemist who is *doing* chemistry and the chemist who brackets that and asks what chemistry is for, who it serves, and why? What are the assumptions that make chemistry work? What are chemistry's potential blind-spots? All of those questions are ignored to some extent when the chemist does chemistry. The phenomenological attitude toward chemistry seems to happen "off the clock," so to speak. I am reminded of Plato's *Republic,* of the ship's captain who constantly gazes at the stars; to the sailors, the captain seems to be a useless dreamer, but they do not know that a ship cannot be steered without first looking to the stars, assessing where one is, and seeking a path.[37] Perhaps orientation *requires* disorientation. Like the captain in Plato's *Republic,* our own lives are guided by philosophical questions (and answers), whether we consciously ask them or not. It is disorienting to consciously ask these questions, to bring them from the netherworlds to the forefront of our thinking. Louis Althusser would say that, in defining ideology, we are always already on a path (engaged in an orientation) until we learn to question it. To raise philosophical questions about your orientation is to put your position on the ship at risk, for the "civilized" sailors may misinterpret your disorientation.

Adam Phillips talks about the failure of "getting it"[38] (see chapter 2) and Judith Butler discusses how "one undergoes a decentering and 'fails' to achieve self-identity."[39] Luckily, "failure" and decentering are everywhere, since no one can ever perfectly fit into a social role provided for them. And these experiences of not fitting are our opportunities to stretch ourselves. We can actively think, or we can turn off our thinking. The first mode is the mode of critique and, indeed, the mode of maturing.

The problem is as Freud has laid it out: There are social benefits to not thinking. This is what Althusser deems ideology, and society celebrates us when we live according to ideology. This is often literal celebration. A person may know rationally that nations are violent structures of war, hierarchy, and exclusion, and yet still celebrate the Fourth of July; they may know rationally that marriage is a patriarchal institution based on the exchange of women as objects and yet still get married. Even when one is in the minority and aware of the ethical wrong of the ideological celebration, one tends to "go along." Under tight social controls, going along seems the only way to have connections, friends, family, camaraderie, and fun. Social control as civilization is precisely this fear that if one acts on one's ethics, one will have no friends. And, what is more, "the intellectual and emotional refusal 'to go along' appears as neurotic and impotent" within a social fabric where "technological control" and total administration "appear to be the very embodiment of Reason."[40]

We should not mistake such "going along" as ethics. Against Freud, let us recognize that ethics requires us to critique civilization. There are really two problems here: one, that many people never learn to develop the intellectual skills of critique; and, two, that even those who do develop those skills too often use them only intellectually and not *practically and materially*—they do not change their behavior in keeping with their critique. Critique cannot remain a mere intellectual game; it must move out into the world, and for this people need to kick social control as a mandate of civilized behavior to the curb. This is going to require a level of courage that capitalist societies constantly tell us we do not have.

Another invitation to critical openness can be found in honest friendship. To return to Ahmed for a moment, she claims that there is a relationship between queerness and support: "The queer body is not alone; queer does not reside in a body or object, and is dependent on the mutuality of support."[41] But we also know that the ground (the context of the world) does not support all people equally; therefore, in Ahmed's words, "When we tread on paths that are less trodden . . . we might need more support." Some people need more support than others, suggesting Marx's famous idea, "From each according to his ability, to each according to his needs."

This seems right to me. But how should we define "support"? Is it merely positive, affirmational? If so, then perhaps Ahmed is right that traditionally oppressed groups will definitely need more support, as the ground does not support their lives, choices, or flourishing. But support can also be challenge. In this sense, we support a person's move toward the openness of maturing. I think this is often the kind of support teachers give students by challenging them and assigning them readings that they do not think they are capable of understanding. When they try amid others, they find that they *are* capable. Likewise, this can occur in a friendship when we share our experiences, challenge our friends on their ideas and beliefs, and question our own beliefs. In an honest friendship between a man and a woman, for instance, the woman could help her friend to see the daily injustices of being a woman. A man who does not experience this particular disorientation could, through love for his friend, begin to see and experience the world as she does. Like Aristotle, I would argue that this is one of the tasks of a true friend, to help us see the world the way that they do and to expand our narrow view of what subjectivity is. When I begin to see the world as my friend sees it, I am not only liable to be disoriented by what occurs to me but by what disorients my friend, too.

Support, therefore, needs to be both affirmative and challenging. In Augustine's book *Against the Academicians*, he says that wealth is a "seductive whirlpool" because it may lead you to live a life surrounded by fake honors, fancy buildings, and yes-men posing as friends.[42] Augustine is tutoring a young privileged boy and asks him, "Well, I ask you, who, Romanianus, who would dare to mention to you another happy life—one that alone is the happy life?"[43] Who could persuade you that you were living an inauthentic and unhappy life? Who could persuade you that your friends are not real friends and that they are not helping you to find truth?[44] Such people will often not mature, will not be open, and their beliefs or experience of the world will likely go unchallenged. People who merely agree with you, support you without critique, and give you nothing but "positive vibes" are not true friends. They are not helping you to develop as a person, to incorporate more of the world into yourself. Friends disorient us; when it is time to grow, they let us know. Honest friendship requires what Michel Foucault calls *parrhesia,*[45] truth-speaking that involves risk. This brings us back to a key point from Hegel: Dialogue involves antithesis. The person who will not hear or accept disagreement is what Hegel calls the "good conscience"[46] in that they only want to hear what fits their preconceived notion of how the world works and who they are. So let us support one another, not only in how we are but in how we *might be.* Like Tsing's mushrooms, the future calls for us to develop a different type of environmental support, in fact a different conception of maturing altogether.

This book began with a question, "What is maturity?" and ends with more questions. We have come to recognize, I hope, some of the things that maturity should *not* be. But what it will become remains for us to work on collectively. The idea that this concept is an "it"—a thing, a stage, a level to reach—is itself a problem. Maturing is more of an attitude, an orientation toward the world, than it is a goal. When I understand myself to be entwined with others, I also understand that I am not only responsible for my own orientation but for yours and ours as well. To orient ourselves toward critical openness is to give up the hope of a unified self, an autonomous self. We co-orient and dis-orient each other in the polis.

NOTES

1. Emanuel Levinas, *Time and the Other*, trans. Richard A. Cohen (Pittsburgh: Duquesne University Press, 1994).
2. Levinas, *Time and the Other*, 105.
3. Levinas, *Time and the Other*, 107.
4. Epicurus, "Letter to Menoeceus," trans. Cyril Bailey, https://users.manchester.edu/Facstaff/SSNaragon/Online/texts/316/Epicurus,%20LetterMenoeceus.pdf.
5. Judith Butler, *Giving an Account of Oneself* (New York: Fordham University Press, 2005), 8.
6. Douglas Kellner, "Introduction to the Second Edition," in Herbert Marcuse, *One-Dimensional Man: Studies in the Ideology of Advanced Industrial Society* (Boston: Beacon Press, 1991), xiv–xv.
7. Sara Ahmed, *Queer Phenomenology: Orientations, Objects, Others* (Durham: Duke University Press, 2006), 1.
8. Ahmed, *Queer Phenomenology*, 157.
9. Ahmed, *Queer Phenomenology*, 157.
10. Ahmed, *Queer Phenomenology*, 158.
11. Noel Ignatiev, *How the Irish Became White* (New York: Routledge, 1995).
12. Christa Hodapp, *Men's Rights, Gender, and Social Media* (Lanham: Lexington Books, 2017).
13. Ahmed, *Queer Phenomenology*, 159.
14. Ahmed, *Queer Phenomenology*, 160.
15. Simone de Beauvoir, *The Second Sex*, trans. Constance Borde and Sheila Malovany-Chevallier (New York: Vintage Books, 2011).
16. Herbert Marcuse, *One-Dimensional Man: Studies in the Ideology of Advanced Industrial Society* (Boston: Beacon Press, 1991), 9.
17. Marcuse, *One-Dimensional Man*, 11.
18. Terry Eagleton, *Ideology: An Introduction* (New York: Verso, 2007), xxiii.
19. Jodi Dean, *Crowds and Party* (New York: Verso, 2006), 58.
20. Dean, *Crowds and Party*, 59.
21. Dean, *Crowds and Party*, 58.
22. Dean, *Crowds and Party*, 57.
23. Dean, *Crowds and Party*, 59.
24. Dean, *Crowds and Party*, 62–63.
25. Dean, *Crowds and Party*, 62–63.
26. Dean, *Crowds and Party*, 63.
27. Marcuse, *One-Dimensional Man*, 10.
28. Marcuse, *One-Dimensional Man*, 244–45.
29. Marcuse, *One-Dimensional Man*, 10.
30. Marcuse, *One-Dimensional Man*, 245.
31. Ahmed, *Queer Phenomenology*, 159.
32. Maurice Merleau-Ponty, *Phenomenology of Perception*, trans. Colin Smith (London: Routledge Classics, 2002), xv.

33. Edmund Husserl, "The Vienna Lecture," in *The Continental Philosophy Reader*, ed. Richard Kearney and Mara Rainwater (New York: Routledge, 1996), 7–14.

34. Edmund Husserl, *Psychological and Transcendental Phenomenology and the Confrontation with Heidegger (1927–1931)*, ed. and trans. Thomas Sheehan and Richard E. Palmer (Dordrecht, The Netherlands: Kluwer Academic Publishers, 1997), 179.

35. Brandon Absher, *The Rise of Neoliberal Philosophy: Human Capital, Profitable Knowledge, and the Love of Wisdom* (Lanham: Lexington Books, 2021).

36. Ahmed, *Queer Phenomenology*, 159.

37. Plato, *Republic*, trans. C. D. C. Reeve (Indianapolis: Hackett Publishing Company, 1992).

38. Adam Phillips, *Missing Out: In Praise of the Unlived Life* (New York: Farrar, Straus and Giroux, 2013).

39. Butler, *Giving an Account of Oneself*, 42.

40. Marcuse, *One-Dimensional Man*, 9.

41. Ahmed, *Queer Phenomenology*, 170.

42. Augustine, *Against the Academicians*, trans. Peter King (Indianapolis: Hackett Publishing, 1997).

43. Augustine, *Against the Academicians*, 3.

44. Augustine, *Against the Academicians*, 3.

45. Michel Foucault, *Fearless Speech*, ed. Joseph Pearson (Cambridge: MIT Press, 2001).

46. Georg Wilhelm Friedrich Hegel, *Phenomenology of Spirit*, trans. A. V. Miller (Oxford: Oxford University Press, 1977).

Bibliography

Absher, Brandon. *The Rise of Neoliberal Philosophy: Human Capital, Profitable Knowledge, and the Love of Wisdom.* Lanham: Lexington Books, 2021.

Ahmed, Sara. *Queer Phenomenology: Orientations, Objects, Others.* Durham: Duke University Press, 2006.

Althusser, Louis. *Writings on Psychoanalysis: Freud and Lacan.* New York: Columbia University Press, 1996.

Altman, Neil. *Psychoanalysis in an Age of Accelerating Cultural Change: Spiritual Globalization.* New York: Routledge, 2015. Quoted in Scott Graybow, *Progressive Psychoanalysis as a Social Justice Movement*. Newcastle upon Tyne, UK: Cambridge Scholars Publishing, 2017.

Arendt, Hannah. "Thinking and Moral Considerations: A Lecture." *Social Research* 38, no. 3 (Autumn 1971): 417–46. https://www.jstor.org/stable/40970069.

Arrupe, Pedro. "Men for Others: Training Agents of Change for the Promotion of Justice; Father Arrupe's Address to the International Congress of Jesuit Alumni of Europe, Valencia, Spain, July 31, 1973." In *Justice with Faith Today: Selected Letters and Addresses—II*, edited by Jerome Aixala, 123–38. St. Louis: The Institute of Jesuit Sources, 1980. https://jesuitportal.bc.edu/research/documents/1973_arrupemenforothers/.

Augustine. *Against the Academicians.* Translated by Peter King. Indianapolis: Hackett Publishing, 1997.

Balibar, Etienne. *Citizen Subject: Foundations of Philosophical Anthropology.* New York: Fordham University Press, 2017.

Bawer, Bruce. *A Place at the Table: The Gay Individual in American Society.* New York: Simon & Schuster, 1994. Quoted in Sara Ahmed, *Queer Phenomenology: Orientations, Objects, Others.* Durham: Duke University Press, 2006.

Beauvoir, Simone de. *The Second Sex*. Translated by Constance Borde and Sheila Malovany-Chevallier. New York: Vintage Books, 2011.

Bhattacharya, Tithi. "Introduction: Mapping Social Reproduction Theory." In *Social Reproduction Theory: Remapping Class, Recentering Oppression,* edited by Tithi Bhattacharya, 1–20. London: Pluto Press, 2017.

Blanchot, Maurice. *Friendship.* Translated by Elizabeth Rottenberg. Stanford: Stanford University Press, 1997.

———. *The Book to Come.* Translated by Charlotte Mandell. Stanford: Stanford University Press, 2003.

———. *The Space of Literature.* Translated by Ann Smock. Lincoln: University of Nebraska Press, 1982.

Bobbio, Norberto. *Liberalism and Democracy.* New York: Verso Books, 2005.

Brown, Norman O. *Life Against Death: The Psychoanalytical Meaning of History.* Middletown: Wesleyan University Press, 1959.

———. *Love's Body.* New York: Random House, 1966.

Butler, Judith. *Giving an Account of Oneself.* New York: Fordham University Press, 2005.

———. *Precarious Life: The Powers of Mourning and Violence.* London: Verso, 2004.

Carrington, Damian. "'Our Leaders Are Like Children,' School Strike Founder Tells Climate Summit." *The Guardian*, December 4, 2018. https://www.theguardian.com/environment/2018/dec/04/leaders-like-children-school-strike-founder-greta-thunberg-tells-un-climate-summit.

Chodorow, Nancy J. *Feminism and Psychoanalytic Theory.* New Haven: Yale University Press, 1989.

Davis, Angela Y. *Women, Race and Class.* New York: Vintage Books, 1983.

Dean, Jodi. *Crowds and Party.* New York: Verso, 2006.

Deleuze, Gilles. *The Fold: Leibniz and the Baroque*. Translated by Tom Conley. London: Athlone Press, 1993.

Derrida, Jacques. "Force of Law: The Mystical Foundation of Authority." In *Deconstruction and the Possibility of Justice*, edited by Drucilla Cornell, Michel Rosenfeld, and David Gray Carlson, 3–67. New York: Routledge, 1992.

Dickson, E.J. "Why Are Judges so Concerned About the Future of Potential Rapists?" *Rolling Stone*, July 19, 2019. https://www.rollingstone.com/culture/culture-features/judge-james-troiano-brock-turner-sexual-assault-855415/.

Dinshaw, Carolyn, Lee Edelman, Roderick A. Ferguson, Carla Freccero, Elizabeth Freeman, Judith Halberstam, Annamarie Jagose, Christopher Nealon, and Nguyen Tan Hoang. "Theorizing Queer Temporalities: A Roundtable Discussion." *GLQ: A Journal of Lesbian and Gay Studies* 13, no. 2–3 (2007): 177–95. doi:10.1215/10642684-2006-030.

Eagleton, Terry. *Ideology: An Introduction.* New York: Verso, 2007.

Edelman, Lee. *No Future: Queer Theory and the Death Drive.* Durham: Duke University Press, 2004.

Epicurus. "Letter to Menoeceus." Translated by Cyril Bailey. https://users.manchester.edu/Facstaff/SSNaragon/Online/texts/316/Epicurus,%20LetterMenoeceus.pdf.

Fanon, Frantz. *Black Skin, White Masks.* New York: Grove Press, 1967.

———. *The Wretched of the Earth.* New York: Grove Press, 1963.

Federici, Silvia. *Caliban and the Witch: Women, the Body and Primitive Accumulation.* New York: Autonomedia, 2004.

———. *Witches, Witch-Hunting, and Women.* San Francisco: PM Press, 2018.

Ferguson, Susan. "Children, Childhood and Capitalism: A Social Reproduction Perspective." In *Social Reproduction Theory: Remapping Class, Recentering Oppression,* edited by Tithi Bhattacharya, 112–30. London: Pluto Press, 2017.

Field, Connie, dir. *The Life and Times of Rosie the Riveter*. 1980; Berkeley, CA: Clarity Films, 2014. DVD.

Firestone, Shulamith. *The Dialectic of Sex: The Case for Feminist Revolution.* New York: Macmillan, 1970.

Fisher, Mark. *Capitalist Realism: Is There No Alternative?* Winchester: Zero Books, John Hunt Publishing, 2009.

Foucault, Michel. *Fearless Speech.* Edited by Joseph Pearson. Cambridge: MIT Press, 2001.

Fraser, Nancy. "Crisis of Care? On the Social-Reproductive Contradictions of Contemporary Capitalism." In *Social Reproduction Theory: Remapping Class, Recentering Oppression,* edited by Tithi Bhattacharya, 21–36. London: Pluto Press, 2017.

Freud, Sigmund. *Civilization and Its Discontents*. Translated and edited by James Strachey. New York: W.W. Norton, 1962.

———. *The Interpretation of Dreams*. Translated by A.A. Brill. Hertfordshire, UK: Wordsworth Editions Limited, 1997.

———. "Three Contributions to the Theory of Sex." In *The Basic Writings of Sigmund Freud,* translated and edited by A.A. Brill, 521–600. New York: The Modern Library, 1995.

Gavey, Nicola. *Just Sex? The Cultural Scaffolding of Rape.* New York: Routledge, 2019.

Graybow, Scott. *Progressive Psychoanalysis as a Social Justice Movement.* Newcastle upon Tyne, UK: Cambridge Scholars Publishing, 2017.

Halberstam, J. *In a Queer Place and Time: Transgender Bodies, Subcultural Lives.* New York: New York University Press, 2005. Quoted in Sara Ahmed, *Queer Phenomenology: Orientations, Objects, Others.* Durham: Duke University Press, 2006.

———. *The Queer Art of Failure.* Durham: Duke University Press, 2011.

Haraway, Donna J. *Manifestly Haraway.* Minneapolis: University of Minnesota Press, 2016.

———. *Staying with the Trouble: Making Kin in the Chthulucene.* Durham: Duke University Press, 2016.

———. *The Haraway Reader.* New York: Routledge, 2004.

Hegel, Georg Wilhelm Friedrich. *Phenomenology of Spirit.* Translated by A.V. Miller. Oxford: Oxford University Press, 1977.

Hira, Sandew. "A Decolonial Critique of the Concept of White Privilege: Why Injustice is Not a Privilege." *Decolonial International Network,* 2017. https://din.today/a-decolonial-critique-of-the-concept-of-white-privilege-why-injustice-is-not-a-privilege/.

Hodapp, Christa. *Men's Rights, Gender, and Social Media.* Lanham: Lexington Books, 2017.

Hondo, Med, director. *Soleil Ô (Oh, Sun)*. France / Mauritania, 1970. 1 hr., 44 min. Screened at the 2020 Berlin International Film Festival. https://www.berlinale.de/en/archive-selection/archive-2020/programme/detail/202012225.html.

Husserl, Edmund. *Psychological and Transcendental Phenomenology and the Confrontation with Heidegger (1927–1931)*. Translated and edited by Thomas Sheehan and Richard E. Palmer. Dordrecht, The Netherlands: Kluwer Academic Publishers, 1997.

———. "The Vienna Lecture." In *The Continental Philosophy Reader*, edited by Richard Kearney and Mara Rainwater, 7–14. New York: Routledge, 1996.

Ignatiev, Noel. *How the Irish Became White.* New York: Routledge, 1995.

Johnson, Jake. "House Progressives Hail Biden Moves to Combat Meat Industry 'Price Gouging.'" *Common Dreams*, January 4, 2022. https://www.commondreams.org/news/2022/01/04/house-progressives-hail-biden-moves-combat-meat-industry-price-gouging.

Kellner, Douglas. "Introduction to the Second Edition." In Herbert Marcuse, *One-Dimensional Man: Studies in the Ideology of Advanced Industrial Society,* xiv–xv. Boston: Beacon Press, 1991.

Klein, Avi. "Opinion: What Men Say About #MeToo in Therapy." *New York Times,* June 30, 2018. https://www.nytimes.com/2018/06/30/opinion/sunday/men-metoo-therapy-masculinity.html.

Kristeva, Julia. *Intimate Revolt: The Powers and Limits of Psychoanalysis.* Translated by Jeanine Herman. New York: Columbia University Press, 2002.

———. "Women's Time." Translated by Alice Jardine and Harry Blake. In *The Kristeva Reader*, edited by Toril Moi, 187–213. New York: Columbia, 1986.

Lacan, Jacques. "The Mirror Stage as Formative of the *I* Function as Revealed in Psychoanalytic Experience." In *Écrits: The First Complete Edition in English*, translated by Bruce Fink, 75–81. New York: W.W. Norton and Company, 2006.

Levinas, Emmanuel. *Existence and Existents.* Translated by Alphonso Lingis. Dordrecht: Kluwer Academic Press, 1995.

———. *Time and the Other*. Translated by Richard A. Cohen. Pittsburgh: Duquesne University Press, 1994.

Lewis, Sophie. *Full Surrogacy Now: Feminism Against Family.* London: Verso Books, 2021.

Marcuse, Herbert. *Marxism, Revolution and Utopia: Collected Papers of Herbert Marcuse, Volume 6*. Edited by Douglas Kellner and Clayton Pierce. New York: Routledge, 2014.

———. *One-Dimensional Man: Studies in the Ideology of Advanced Industrial Society.* Boston: Beacon Press, 1991.

Marx, Karl. "Estranged Labor." In *Economic and Philosophic Manuscripts of 1844*. https://www.marxists.org/archive/marx/works/1844/manuscripts/labour.htm.

McIntosh, Peggy. "White Privilege: Unpacking the Invisible Knapsack." *Peace and Freedom Magazine* (July/August 1989): 10–12. https://psychology.umbc.edu/files/2016/10/White-Privilege_McIntosh-1989.pdf.

McLeary, Jairus, and Gethin Aldous, directors. *The Work.* Blanketfort Media, 2017. 1 hr., 29 min.

Merleau-Ponty, Maurice. *Phenomenology of Perception*. Translated by Donald A. Landes. New York: Routledge, 2012.

Meyer, Robinson. "Dude, She's (Exactly 25 Percent) Out of Your League." *The Atlantic*, August 10, 2018. https://www.theatlantic.com/science/archive/2018/08/online-dating-out-of-your-league/567083/.

Mohandesi, Salar, and Emma Teitelman. "Without Reserves." In *Social Reproduction Theory: Remapping Class, Recentering Oppression,* edited by Tithi Bhattacharya, 37–67. London: Pluto Press, 2017.

Muñoz, José Esteban. *Disidentifications: Queers of Color and the Performance of Politics.* Minneapolis: University of Minnesota Press, 1999.

Murphy, Ann. "The Redress of Psychoanalysis." In *Clinical Encounters in Sexuality: Psychoanalytic Practice and Queer Theory*, edited by Noreen Giffney and Eve Watson, 223–34. Earth, Milky Way: Punctum Books, 2017.

Niccolai, Ivan. Comment on the Facebook page of Jaleh Mansoor, July 10, 2018. Quoted with permission.

Nietzsche, Friedrich. *Beyond Good and Evil: Prelude to a Philosophy of the Future*. Translated and commentary by Walter Kaufmann. New York: Vintage Books, 1989.

Nussbaum, Martha C. *Frontiers of Justice: Disability, Nationality, Species Membership.* Cambridge: Harvard University Press, 2009.

Ortega, Mariana. The 18th Annual Meeting of the Phenomenology Roundtable, San Antonio, TX, May 31–June 2, 2017. https://phenomenologyroundtable.wordpress.com/2017/11/05/18th-annual-phenomenology-roundtable-meeting/.

Phillips, Adam. *Missing Out: In Praise of the Unlived Life.* New York: Farrar, Straus and Giroux, 2013.

———. Week-Long Residency with Adam Phillips at The Center for the Study of Psychoanalysis and Culture, SUNY-Buffalo, 2015.

Rose, Jacqueline. "Something Amiss." In *Clinical Encounters in Sexuality: Psychoanalytic Practice and Queer Theory*, edited by Noreen Giffney and Eve Watson, 391–96. Earth, Milky Way: Punctum Books, 2017.

Ross, Joann M. "Making Marital Rape Visible: A History of American Legal and Social Movements Criminalizing Rape in Marriage." PhD diss., University of Nebraska-Lincoln, 2015. https://digitalcommons.unl.edu/cgi/viewcontent.cgi?article=1085&context=historydiss.

Sanchez, Carlos. "Ortega y Gasset's Existentialist Critique of Husserl's Transcendental Phenomenology." The 15th Annual Meeting of the Phenomenology Roundtable, California State University Fresno, May 24, 2015.

Sears, Alan. "Body Politics: The Social Reproduction of Sexualities." In *Social Reproduction Theory: Remapping Class, Recentering Oppression,* edited by Tithi Bhattacharya, 171–91. London: Pluto Press, 2017.

Shafer, Emily Fitzgibbons. "Hillary Rodham Versus Hillary Clinton: Consequences of Surname Choice in Marriage." *Gender Issues* 34 (2017): 316–32. https://doi.org/10.1007/s12147-016-9182-5.

Shine, Jacqui. "Sympathy for the White Devil: Phoebe Maltz Bovy's 'The Perils of Privilege.'" *Los Angeles Review of Books*, April 16, 2017, https://lareviewofbooks.

org/article/sympathy-for-the-white-devil-phoebe-maltz-bovys-the-perils-of-privilege/.

Smith, Joan. *Misogynies.* London: Westbourne Press, 1989.

Snediker, Michael. "Out of Line, On Hold: D.W. Winnicott's Queer Sensibilities." In *Clinical Encounters in Sexuality: Psychoanalytic Practice and Queer Theory*, edited by Noreen Giffney and Eve Watson, 145–70. Earth, Milky Way: Punctum Books, 2017.

Taylor, Matthew, and Jessica Murray. "'Overwhelming and Terrifying': The Rise of Climate Anxiety." *The Guardian*, February 10, 2020. https://www.theguardian.com/environment/2020/feb/10/overwhelming-and-terrifying-impact-of-climate-crisis-on-mental-health.

Totenberg, Nina, and Sarah McCammon. "Supreme Court Overturns Roe v. Wade, Ending Right to Abortion Upheld for Decades." *All Things Considered*, NPR, June 24, 2022. https://www.npr.org/2022/06/24/1102305878/supreme-court-abortion-roe-v-wade-decision-overturn.

Tsing, Anna Lowenhaupt. *The Mushroom at the End of the World: On the Possibility of Life in Capitalist Ruins.* Princeton: Princeton University Press, 2015.

Veblen, Thorstein. *The Theory of the Leisure Class: An Economic Study of Institutions.* New York: The Macmillan Company, 1912.

Warner, Michael. *The Trouble with Normal: Sex, Politics, and the Ethics of Queer Life*. Cambridge: Harvard University Press, 1999.

Whitehouse, David. "Origins of the Police." Libcom.org, December 24, 2014. https://libcom.org/history/origins-police-david-whitehouse.

Winnicott, Donald Woods. *Playing and Reality.* New York: Routledge Classics, 2005.

Young, Iris Marion. *Justice and the Politics of Difference.* Princeton: Princeton University Press, 1990.

Index

abortion, 66–67, 75, 80, 82
activist, 3–4, 20, 37, 60, 62, 80, 82
adolescence, 21–22; idealism of, 22, 25
"adulting," 18, 22
adults, 26, 36, 47; children treated as, 74; colonizers as, 53; ecological crisis and, 60; Freud on, 11, 22, 32; normative conceptions of, 4–5, 18, 23–24, 36, 38–41, 61; play and, 15, 18, 74–75, 83; Winnicott on, 14–15, 18–20, 22
Against the Academicians (Augustine), 98
Ahmed, Sara: critique of normative cultural expectations, 5, 41; on disorientation, 89–91, 95–96; on melancholy, 58; on queerness and support, 97
alienation, 21, 79, 82, 92
Althusser, Louis, 3–4, 96
Altman, Neil, 10
anaclitic love. *See* love
Anthropocene, 81–82
antisocial, 40
apolitical negativity. *See* negativity
the Apollonian and Dionysian, 32
Arbery, Ahmaud, 37
Arendt, Hannah, 5
Aristotle, 2, 98
Augustine, 98
autonomy, 21, 23, 55, 92–95

Balibar, Etienne, 13, 51–52
Bawer, Bruce, 41
beauty-industrial complex, 19
Beauvoir, Simone de, 3, 13, 57, 71, 91
Beyond Good and Evil: Prelude to a Philosophy of the Future (Nietzsche), 1, 27
Biden, Joe, 61
The Birds (Hitchcock), 39
birth control, 67, 80, 82. *See also* contraception
Black culture. *See* culture
Black liberation, 51
Black Lives Matter movement, 37
Blackness, 51
Black people, 37, 43, 47–49, 51–54, 57, 67, 69, 88, 91
Black Skin, White Masks (Fanon), 51
Blanchot, Maurice: on death and art, 31–35, 40; on failure and success, 35–38, 42–43; on negativity, 38, 40–43
Bobbio, Norberto, 22–23
"Body Politics: The Social Reproduction of Sexualities" (Sears), 72

bourgeois, 24, 42, 67–69, 74–76, 78, 81, 93
Brown, Norman O., 19, 31–32
Butler, Judith, 55, 71, 89, 96

capitalism: alienation and, 21, 82, 92–94; children and, 78–79; family and, 6, 65, 68, 70, 72, 76, 78–79; environment and, 60–61, 82–83; health and, 10, 59–62; history of, 67–69, 70, 73, 76; industrialization and, 68–69, 73; late, 10, 25–26, 32, 36, 60–62, 67, 74, 76, 78, 97; maturity and, 5–6, 21, 59, 61, 92–93; (neo)liberalism and, 10, 22–23, 83; patriarchy and, 67–68, 70, 72, 76–77, 92–93; violence and, 53–54, 67–68, 74, 77; witch trials and, 53–54, 67–68
Capitalist Realism (Fisher), 59–62
capitalist realism, critical reflection and, 59–62
caregivers, 16, 20, 76
celebration, 65, 69, 77, 82–83, 96–97
Césaire, Aimé, 53
The Child, 38–40
childhood, 12, 22, 35, 41–43, 56, 72–74, 76, 78, 81
child labor, 76
children: adults behaving like, 4, 41, 60; bourgeois family values and, 5, 65, 69–70, 73, 75–79; capitalism and, 78–79; colonized peoples treated as, 53, 55, 57; Freud on, 21–22; historical treatment of, 65, 67–68, 73–75; indigenous, 67, 80; raising, 26, 38–39, 65, 83; Winnicott on, 18–20
"Children, Childhood and Capitalism: A Social Reproduction Perspective" (Ferguson), 78
Chodorow, Nancy, 32
Citizen Subject: Foundations of Philosophical Anthropology (Balibar), 51
class, 4–5, 7, 8n17, 10, 40, 47, 49–50, 76, 57, 59, 67–72, 74–76, 78, 80, 82–83
class consciousness, 58, 60
climate: activism, 60, 80; anxiety, 60–61; catastrophe, 60, 79; change, 60, 82; crisis, 2, 60, 67; justice, 80
Clinton, Bill, 38–39
closedness, 6, 87–90, 92
cognitive behavioral therapy (CBT). *See* therapy
collectivity, 4, 93, 95
colonization, 52–54, 81
communism, 22–23, 77–78
contraception, 66. *See also* birth control
creativity, 5, 17–19
"Crisis of Care?" (Fraser), 76
critical openness, 87–98
critical theory, 3, 48, 75, 80
culture, 7, 12, 25, 38, 49, 57, 59, 68–70, 76–78, 81, 91, 94; Black, 51; modern, 24–26, 36, 39–40, 47; heteronormative, 38; hustle, 25; management, 61; queer, 41–42; rape, 72; White, 51; Winnicott on, 15–17, 19–20

Davis, Angela, 57, 67
Davis, Vaginal Creme, 43
Dean, Jodi, 93
death, 22, 31, 33–34, 39–40, 55–56, 65, 87–88
death drive, 38–40
Deleuze, Gilles, 4
Derrida, Jacques, 6–7, 38
The Dialectic of Sex: The Case for Feminist Revolution (Firestone), 66, 71
disenfranchised, 53
Disidentifications: Queers of Color and the Performance of Politics (Muñoz), 43
disorientation, 59, 89–91, 93, 95–96, 98
Du Bois, W. E. B., 81

Eagleton, Terry, 92
Earth kin. *See* kin
eco-anxiety, 60
eco-catastrophe, 67
Edelman, Lee, 38–41
ego, 11–13, 16, 19–20, 22, 31, 34, 48, 88
Engels, Friedrich, 66
Epicurus, 88
Eros, 31–32
essentialism, 14, 16, 22, 69–70, 82
ethical heterosexuality, 71
ethics, 2, 26–27, 32, 47, 87–89, 97; virtue, 2, 59
Existence and Existents (Levinas), 34

the "face," 20, 88
failure: as critique of identity norms, 43; Blanchot on, 34–36, 42; fear of, 15; immaturity as, 38, 43; praise of, 42; queer theory on, 38–43; social roles and, 26, 43, 65–66, 70, 96
familia, 65, 74
family, 2, 5, 22, 24, 41–42, 56, 60, 65–70, 72–77, 79, 81, 83, 97
family love. *See* love
famulus, 65, 74
Fanon, Frantz, 51–53, 91
Federici, Silvia, 53–54, 67–68, 77
femininity, 68, 70–71
Ferguson, Susan, 78
the "five faces of oppression," 47–48
Firestone, Shulamith, 3, 65–66, 71–76, 78
Fisher, Mark, 59–62
Floyd, George, 37
"fold," 4
Foucault, Michel, 98
Fraser, Nancy, 76
Freud, Sigmund, 9–10, 19; children and, 21–22; on ethics, 88–89, 96–97; and the id-ego-superego, 11–12, 31–32, 48, 87; on love, 24; on the maturing process, 10–14, 25; on sexuality's role in maturity, 12–14
friction, 16–17
Full Surrogacy Now: Feminism Against Family (Lewis), 66–67, 83
futurism, reproductive, 38–40

games, 74–75
gender roles, 14, 55–57, 66–70
gene fetish, 70, 73, 75
genetic progeny, obsession with, 73
"getting it," 26, 96
Gilman, Charlotte Perkins, 81
Giving an Account of Oneself (Butler), 89
global warming, 60–61, 66–67, 83
the "good conscience," 98
"good family," 5, 8n17
Graybow, Scott, 10

Halberstam, Jack, 5, 40–43, 57
Haraway, Donna, 1, 80–83
Hardt, Michael, 93
health, 9–10, 16, 18–20, 23, 59–61, 70–72
healthcare, 10, 37, 59, 82
health problems, late capitalism and, 61
Hegel, Georg Wilhelm Friedrich, 31–33, 43, 50–52, 55, 57, 92, 98
Henry VIII of England, 73
heteronormativity, 38, 40, 69–72, 91
heterosexual, 5, 12, 14, 42, 49, 57–58, 69–73, 81
Hondo, Med, 54
Husserl, Edmund, 95–96
hustle culture. *See* culture

id, 11–12, 31–32, 48
idealism, 14, 22, 25, 38
identification, 20–21, 54, 58
ideology, 1, 4, 6, 40, 54, 58, 71, 88, 92–94, 96–97; family, 65–69; patriarchal, 75, 82
immaturity, 3, 5–7, 14–15, 19–20, 22–23, 36, 40, 62, 89, 93; failure and, 31, 38, 43; queer theory on, 38–43

industrialization, 68–69, 73
injustice, 27, 47–48, 53, 97
The Interpretation of Dreams (Freud), 21–22

justice, 2, 6, 10, 17, 26, 47–48, 74, 80, 82–83, 87, 95
Justice and the Politics of Difference (Young), 47–48

Kafka, Franz, 33, 35
Kellner, Douglas, 89
kin, 54, 79–80, 83; Earth, 79, 83
kinship, 67, 81, 83
Kristeva, Julia, 11, 56–57
Kundera, Milan, 58–59

Lacan, Jacques, 20, 23, 26–27, 38
Levinas, Emmanuel, 25–27, 34, 87–89
Lewis, Sophie, 66–67, 79, 83
LGBT, 42
liberal (neoliberal), 10, 22–23, 49, 83, 93–94
Liberalism and Democracy (Bobbio), 22–23
listening, 36, 48
"lord and bondsman" dialectic, 52, 55. *See also* master-slave dialectic
love, 2, 5, 13, 17, 24, 42, 56, 58–59, 65, 71–73, 77, 79, 90, 94–95, 98; anaclitic, 24; family, 5

management culture. *See* culture
Marcuse, Herbert, 6, 24–25, 31–32, 60, 78, 89, 92, 94
marriage, 5, 18, 38, 41–42, 65–70, 73–74, 77, 79, 97
Marx, Karl, 21, 60, 66, 79, 97
Marxist, 57, 60, 70, 76, 78
masculinity, 55–56, 93
master-slave dialectic, 50–51. *See also* "lord and bondsman" dialectic
materialism, 4
maturity, 1–7, 8n17, 9–27, 31–32, 35–38, 41–43, 47–53, 56–57, 59–62, 65, 72, 76, 78, 81, 83, 89–93, 95–98; activism and, 37; capitalism and, 59–62, 92–93; disorientation and, 90; ethics and, 89; family and, 65; Freud on, 10–14; identification and, 20; immaturity and, 3–4, 6–7, 15, 20, 22–23, 43, 93; individualism and, 93, 95; normative, 2, 5, 7, 14, 18, 36–38, 41–42, 62, 90; openness and, 91, 93, 96–98; oppression and, 49–53; philosophy and, 1–2, 10; play and, 15–19, 21, 78; political issue of, 4, 14, 38, 47, 57, 59–62, 83; provisional definition of, 4–6; psychoanalysis and, 9–10; sexuality's role in, 13–14; Winnicott on, 14–22, 25
McIntosh, Peggy, 48–49
mental health, 10, 59–61
Merleau-Ponty, Maurice, 18, 59, 95
#MeToo, 4
the "mirror stage," 20, 23
Misogynies (Smith), 58
the "mother," 15–16, 20. *See also* caregivers
motherhood, 67, 82
Muñoz, José Esteban, 38, 42–43
Murphy, Ann, 14
The Mushroom at the End of the World: On the Possibility of Life in Capitalist Ruins (Tsing), 82

Native peoples, 47, 54, 67, 80
"negative thinking," 89
negativity, 33, 39–43, 51; apolitical, 40–41, 43
Negri, Antonio, 93
neurotic, 19–20, 97
Nietzsche, Friedrich, 1, 27, 31
No Future: Queer Theory and the Death Drive (Edelman), 38–40
normative maturity. *See* maturity
"not getting it," 24, 26–27
Nussbaum, Martha, 24

One-Dimensional Man: Studies in the Ideology of Advanced Industrial Society (Marcuse), 6, 92
openness, 6–7, 11, 13, 15, 19–20, 24, 26–27, 31, 42–43, 48–49, 56, 65, 80; critical, 89–98; ethical, 88–89
oppression, 4, 10, 27, 47–49, 53, 57–58, 71, 73, 75–76, 90–91, 97; romanticization of, 49–53, 55
Ortega, Mariana, 49–50
the Other, 26, 32, 35, 55, 87–89
otherness, 24, 32, 34–35, 50, 52, 94

parrhesia, 98
patriarchy, 56, 65–67, 69–70, 72–76, 82, 91–93, 97
phenomenology, 36, 55, 58, 89, 95–96
Phenomenology of Spirit (Hegel), 55
Phillips, Adam, 1, 24–26, 96
philosophy, 1–3, 6, 13–14, 22, 31, 34, 37, 47, 49, 56, 58–59, 66, 70, 75, 80–82, 87, 93, 95–96; maturity and, 1–2, 10, 20; psychoanalysis and, 9, 19
A Place at the Table: The Gay Individual in American Society (Bawer), 41
play, 14, 16–19, 21, 31–32, 34, 40, 74–75, 78, 83
Playing and Reality (Winnicott), 14–22, 59
police, 37, 48, 88
positivism, 10
positivist psychology, 9–10
Precarious Life: The Powers of Mourning and Violence (Butler), 55
pregnancy, 73, 82; oppression and, 73
privilege, 4, 47–53, 56, 98
"progress," 2–3, 43, 81
Progressive Psychoanalysis as a Social Justice Movement (Graybow), 10
protest, 37, 47–48
psychoanalysis, 2–4, 9–11, 14–16, 19–20, 26–27, 38, 70
psychotic, 19–20

queer, 38–43, 53, 56, 58–59, 67, 72, 90–91, 95, 97
The Queer Art of Failure (Halberstam), 40
queerness, 38–39, 41, 71, 95, 97
Queer Phenomenology: Orientations, Objects, Others (Ahmed), 58, 89–91
queer theory, 38

race, 4–5, 7, 10, 19–20, 40, 47, 51, 57–59, 74, 76, 81, 83
racism, 37, 48–49, 54, 67, 69, 80–82, 90; protests against, 37
rape, 5, 8n17, 54–55, 71–72, 77
rape culture. *See* culture
reality, 3, 11, 14–16, 18, 20, 25–26, 32, 34–36, 59–62, 70, 73, 78, 80, 94
reality principle, 11, 32
reciprocity, 59
refugees, 74, 82, 88
refusal, 38, 52, 77, 88, 97
relativism, 42, 88
replication, 5, 8n17
The Republic (Plato), 96
resignation, 25
ritual, 18, 69–70, 83
Rose, Jacqueline, 9, 27
Rousseau, Jean Jacques, 21–22, 94

Sanchez, Carlos, 1
Sandel, Michael, 24
Sears, Alan, 72
The Second Sex (Beauvoir), 57–58
Sedgwick, Eve Kosofsky, 27
self-knowledge, 23
sex class, 71, 76
sexism, 70, 76, 81
Sex Pistols, 40
sexual assault, 8n17, 71–72, 77. *See also* rape
Shepard, Matthew, death of, 39–40
*sinthomo*sexual, 39–40
slavery, 51, 57, 67
Smith, Joan, 58
Snediker, Michael, 27

social reproduction, 77–80. *See also* social reproduction theory
social reproduction theory, 76–78; critique of, 78–80
Social Reproduction Theory: Remapping Class, Recentering Oppression (Bhattacharya), 77
Socrates, 17, 95
Socratic questioning, 95
Soleil Ô (Oh, Sun) (Hondo), 54–55
solidarity, 54, 79, 83, 90
The Space of Literature (Blanchot), 33–35
Staying with the Trouble: Making Kin in the Chthulucene (Haraway), 80, 82–83
success, 2, 7, 15, 25, 36, 38, 49, 61, 71, 92–93
superego, 11–13, 31–32, 48, 87
support, queerness and, 97–98

Taylor, Breonna, 37
teenagers, 21–23, 60, 93
"Theorizing Queer Temporalities: A Roundtable Discussion" (Halberstam), 42
therapy, 4, 10, 16–17, 19–20, 55–56, 62; cognitive behavioral therapy (CBT), 10. *See also* psychotherapy
the "there is" (the *il y a*), 34.
"Three Contributions to the Theory of Sex" (Freud), 14
Thunberg, Greta, 60
Toronto Pig Save, 20–21
transitional object, 15
Trolley Problem, 47
The Trouble with Normal: Sex, Politics, and the Ethics of Queer Life (Warner), 42
Tsing, Anna, 2–3, 81–82, 98
Turkle, Sherry, 93–94
Turner, Brock, 8n17

Veblen, Thorstein, 70
vegan, 80, 83
violence, 39, 55–56; against women, 57, 67–68, 77; the family and, 72, 77
virtue ethics. *See* ethics
vulnerability, 55–56, 88, 91–92

Warner, Michael, 42
White culture. *See* culture
White people, 5, 24, 40, 43, 48–54, 57–59, 67–68, 70, 74–75, 81, 90
"White Privilege: Unpacking the Invisible Knapsack" (McIntosh), 48–49
White supremacy, 43, 91
Winnicott, Donald, 9–10; on adolescence, 22; on ethics, 27; on health, 19, 59; on identification, 20; on maturity and development, 14–17, 19, 20–21, 25, 40, 87; on play, 14–19, 74, 78; on psychoanalysis, 9–10, 15–17, 19–20, 27
witch, 53–54, 67
Witches, Witch-Hunting, and Women (Federici), 67–68
Wollstonecraft, Mary, 51–52
Women, Race and Class (Davis), 57
"Women's Time" (Kristeva), 56–57
The Work (McLeary and Aldous), 55–56, 91–92
The Wretched of the Earth (Fanon), 53

Young, Iris Marion, 47–48

About the Author

Tanya Loughead (PhD, KU Leuven) is a philosopher and activist in Buffalo, NY. She is professor in the Department of Philosophy at Canisius College where she is also president of the AAUP chapter and director of Women & Gender Studies. She primarily studies critical theory and phenomenology and has written on philosophers such as Maurice Blanchot, Simone Weil, Angela Davis, Herbert Marcuse, bell hooks, and Sara Ahmed. Her last book was *Critical University* (Lexington Books, 2015).